TOMORROW TO BE BRAVE

FOR
OUR CHILDREN

KATHLEEN
GERALD
SEAN
MARY

THAT THEY MAY BE WHAT THEIR MOTHER WAS

Why have I sought my path with fervent care,
If not in hope to bring all others there.

GOETHE

Tomorrow To Be Brave

JOHN M. FEEHAN

Cowards die many times before their deaths;
The valiant never taste of death but once.
SHAKESPEARE

1972
THE MERCIER PRESS
DUBLIN and CORK

First published Winter 1972

SBN 85342 300 8

By the same author
AN IRISH PUBLISHER AND HIS WORLD

Acknowledgements
So many kind friends helped me with this book that it would be very difficult to list them all but I owe a very special debt of gratitude to the following who were particularly constructive and helpful: Ann Dillon-Malone, Patrick C. Power, Blanaid Irvine, John Stevens, Gillian Somerville-Large, Spike Hennessy, Eithne Strong, Terry Fitzgerald and Doreen Morehead.

My thanks are also due to the following for permission to quote from copyright material: John B. Keane for his poem in Chapter Five, Mrs. Rhoda Hanaghan for her husband's poem in Chapter Six, A. P. Watt & Son (on behalf of the Trustees of the late Hon. Maurice Baring) for Maurice Baring's poem in Chapter One.

Finally I would like to thank my daughter Mary, Editor of The Mercier Press, for her excellent work on the final manuscript.

Printed in Great Britain by The Anchor Press Ltd,
and bound by Wm. Brendon & Son Ltd,
both of Tiptree, Essex

Preface

I was sitting in a Dublin restaurant, shortly after Mary died, having a cup of tea with a friend, gloomily silent and in the depths of depression. He looked me straight in the eyes across the table:

'Tell me something about her,' he said. 'I only met her once but she made a lasting impression on me.'

I began to talk and talk, and as I did the depression lifted, and without my noticing it, Mary became real again in the words I spoke and in the sentences I uttered. He listened enthralled and spellbound. He knew what I was suffering and trying to overcome. Later, in the street, as we said good-bye, he urged me to write a book about her in the way I had spoken: sincere, truthful and from the heart. It would uplift and inspire thousands, he said, as well as being a powerful therapy for myself. To write a book like this would force me to come to grips with the great realities of life, to see things as she had so clearly seen them, and to grope my way out of the darkness and gloom back into the world of light. With these words he left me.

Back at Longfield I strolled through the woods and fields for hours and days in a contemplative yet perplexed mood. As a publisher I had spent my life telling others how to write. Could I now pass the acid test and write this book myself? Could I really grasp Mary's great qualities, penetrate her inner life, decipher her mystique, and bring her back to life again on a canvas that everyone could see and understand. Could I be honest enough to admit my own failings in our life together, my own insensitivity to her great love? We men can be so selfish and sometimes so cruel. We can ignore the wives who love us and treat them as if they were some adjunct, like a refrigerator, a washing machine or a car; something that will always be there and that never has to be appreciated or thanked. Then one day death will come, and we are suddenly alone, and the pain and the void and the suffering of this aloneness is beyond all telling. We are then ripped asunder by bewildering emotions, and cry in agony to have her back, even for a few moments. But our cries and lamentations come too late. There is a time to love and a time to die, and the time to love is now while she is still alive, the time to die may be just around the corner. Every moment is precious and irreplacable. I wondered could I tell of the heroic way she faced, suffered and endured the long lingering pains of cancer? Life and suffering are senselessly inseparable, and suffering is the most merciless of all realities, yet without it our lives cannot be complete. It is the thermometer of one's character. It can make the average man go under, the egoist become still more egotistical, the hard of heart still more cruel, the small mind become still more treacherous and mean. But suffering is powerless to destroy those great and noble spirits who have expurgated all self-love from their lives. They are the real masters of the world, whether they are rich or poor, famous or unknown. They have on their side the power that finally overcomes everything. It was Dostoevski who said: 'There is only one thing I dread – not to be worthy of my sufferings'. Could I give a true picture of one of these great souls?

A few days later I drove to Ennis, still uncertain, still undecided. Here in this beautiful old-world town of picturesque by-ways and ancient buildings, Mary was born. I wandered aimlessly through the narrow crochety streets, down cobbled laneways with the smell of age, by quaint market squares, past the house where she first saw the world, the river bank where she played as a child and grew up as a young girl, the school where she was taught, the church where she daily knelt to pray. The ceaseless business activities of the town went on just as if she had never existed. Life was for those who were alive, and only forgetfulness and oblivion for those who were dead. I walked out into the country, along the Doora Road, made famous by Merriman in his *Midnight Court*. Together as young lovers we had strolled along this road in the Autumn twilights of the past. At a bridge over the River Fergus I stopped and gazed at the dark flowing water underneath. The last time I had stood on this bridge, a few weeks after we had met, she was with me, arm in arm, our minds overflowing with the long, long thoughts of youth and love and life reaching out in all its fullness towards us. But every hope had now dissolved into pain and sorrow and despair. As I bent over the parapet and gazed pensively into the water, I saw a little primrose floating perilously on the surface. It floated along with the current, in and out through the eddies, quivering over the ripples, grazing past the swaying reeds, round and round the whirlpools and out again, trembling at times but still holding on to the water as it made its hazardous journey towards the estuary where it would sink and be lost for ever amid the debris of time. It reminded me so much of Mary's journey through life, through all its perils and difficulties, a thing of beauty noiselessly gliding onwards to a final inevitable destruction.

I knew then I would have to write this book, even though I did not really know why.

On the long drive home I tried to think of a title, and

although several came to my mind they did not satisfy me. Then I remembered that on the day they laid her body to rest in the little churchyard at Dualla I was surrounded by people, many of whom pressed envelopes into my hands until I had nearly an armful. The pain of reading more of these was beyond me, so when I got home I put them away unopened in a drawer. Some short time later, when I was sending out Mary's memorial letter, I had to go through them. They were almost all Mass cards, but there was one sealed, unaddressed envelope, and when I opened it I found a beautiful, artistic sympathy card. Who put it into my hands at the graveyard I do not know. Inside there was a message written in a clear feminine handwriting. The message was only for my eyes but it ended with the words:

Sean dear, I have no words to tell you what I feel for you to-day. I can only give you an inspiring sentence from an eighteenth century poet, John Armstrong:

Distrust yourself, and sleep before you fight
'Tis not too late to-morrow to be brave.

In these words of hope I found the title for my book.

J.M.F.

8th May 1972.

The Mercier Press,
25, Lower Abbey Street,
Dublin, 1.

Chapter One

I watched you and I knew that I had found
The long-delaying, long-expected Spring;
I knew my heart had found a time to sing;
The strength to soar was in my spirits wing;
That life was full of a triumphant sound,
That death could only be a little thing.

Maurice Baring

It was the morning of Monday, February 15th 1971, cold, grey and cloudy.

I lay still in her bed, my hands clasped behind my head, only moving them to nervously chain-smoke cigarette after cigarette. Throughout the night I waited for a telephone call which I knew would tear my world apart, and which I also knew would bring to an end the love, companionship and joy of a life-time. The world we knew and had built up together was falling asunder, and in those odd moments of half-sleep which came to me during the night, I could see her again, floating around the fringe of my semi-consciousness, gliding as if in slow motion through all the days of our lives. Sometimes I saw her, happy and buoyant, emerging from under the breaking surf on some wild strand on the rocky coast of Clare; other times I thought she was strolling with the children through the woods at Ennistymon, the sunlight breaking through the tall trees, like dawn in some primeval forest; again I imagined I could see her lying on the fore-deck of our sailing boat, the green sea-spray flying over her, quietly enjoying each new crest as it surged across our bows. But then I would awaken sharply to the reality of the empty room and the vacant place, and I would realise it was only an illusion, only a dream.

Her crumpled dressing-gown lay carelessly at the end of the bed; her slippers were on the floor, one turned over on its side; her handkerchief was just showing under the pillow; the book she had been reading turned face downwards on the bedside table. Everything looked as if she had only left the room for a few moments; but I knew in my heart that Mary would never come home again. She had gone forever. Three days before, they took her away in an ambulance to a hospital from which she would never return—to a bed, in a ward, where she was destined to die. We both knew this was the fate awaiting her and we had lived with it for a long time; I with a mixture of hope and fear and cowardice; she with dignity, courage, and perfect calm. Our moment of reality had now arrived.

Shortly after seven o'clock the telephone call came. I let the phone ring for a moment or two before lifting the receiver. I was trembling with fear.

'Is that Captain Feehan?' a female voice at the other end asked.

'Yes,' I whispered, my mouth completely dry.

'This is St. Patrick's Hospital, the Reverend Mother speaking. I am sorry to tell you that your wife died at 4.30 this morning.' There was a pause. Each word had crashed between my eyes like blows from a clenched fist which I was powerless to ward off.

'Thank you,' I murmured weakly.

My heart was thumping wildly.

'She died very peacefully and without pain,' the voice continued. Another pause.

'There is no need for you to come up here now. It is best to let the undertaker look after everything. Shall I phone one for you?'

'Please do,' I said. 'And again, thank you'.

Another pause.

Just as I was about to replace the receiver I heard myself saying: 'Would you be so kind as to take her rings off her finger, and, I would like to have a lock of her hair as a memory.' This came on impulse, it was not premeditated.

'Most certainly I will do that,' the Reverend Mother answered.

'Thank you very much again,' I said as I replaced the receiver with a shaking, clammy hand.

It was all over in a few seconds, this horrifying moment I had been waiting for, since I first learned four years before that Mary had cancer and that she was going to die.

I lay there in a daze, for how long I do not know, unable to grasp the reality, unable to stare the new day in the face, until I realised that in the other rooms our four children were also waiting. All were home since Saturday: Kathleen from Scotland, Gerald from Dublin, Sean from Limerick, and young Mary who lived with us. Three days earlier, I had finally accepted the fact that her life was coming quickly to its close, and I had asked them all to return. There were no outbursts of tears or hysterics when I told them; they reacted calmly, but silently, to something they knew to be certain and inevitable. They were her children, flesh of her flesh, blood of her blood, and they had inherited her courage, dignity and greatness.

'Mammy wouldn't want us to cry,' Kathleen said. 'She was much too brave herself.'

The immediate blow of her death was, to some small

extent, dulled by the many practical things which had to be taken care of. Our relatives and close friends, who were also waiting, had to be telephoned. Young Sean left the house immediately and drove the long journey to Ennis to collect Mary's only sister Eily, who in the past few years had lost her mother, her father, and her husband. Death was certainly not sparing our family. Leonore Sierigk, dear, good Leonore, who was so kind, considerate, and helpful to Mary in the last painful months of her life, came with her car, and almost ran a shuttle-service between the house and the various food, drink, clothes, and flower shops in the city. Rooms had to be rearranged and beds prepared for relatives. Soon a few other close friends arrived to give a helping hand, while others, many others, rang up to ask if there was anything possible they could do. Even acquaintances are so very human and understanding in time of sorrow.

After a short while the undertaker, Willie O'Connor of Coburg Street, arrived. I had always dreaded undertakers as people whom familiarity with death had made cruel and heartless, but this man in the first moments, changed all my preconceived ideas. He was kind, considerate and helpful. With gracious tact and understanding, he went through all the painful details of the funeral, and when these were settled, we composed together the death notice for the newspapers:

> FEEHAN (Cork). On February 15th 1971 at St. Patrick's Hospital, Wellington Rd., Cork, Mary P. Feehan (Director of The Mercier Press) dearly beloved wife of Capt. J. M. Feehan, Lanlyn, Woolhara Park, Cork. Deeply regretted by her sorrowing husband and family. Removal on this (Monday) evening at 7 o'clock to Our Lady of Lourdes Church, Ballinlough, Cork. Requiem Mass at 11 o'clock on to-morrow (Tuesday) morning. Funeral immediately afterwards to Dualla Cemetery, Cashel, Co. Tipperary. House private.

As he left we gave him her blue Child of Mary cloak and white veil. Long before, she had asked to be clothed in these in her coffin; they were the last treasures of her childhood.

Throughout all these activities, I tried to be as matter-of-fact as I could, but when the undertaker had left, I began to experience the first real sensations of void and emptiness; everything seemed to have lost its meaning and I wanted to be alone, to be separate, to be by myself, with my thoughts and memories of her.

I went back to her room where I had spent the last few restless nights, and sat on the armchair by her bedside, where I had sat so often and for so long, during those months of anguish as I watched death creep slowly nearer and nearer, day by day. It was sitting here that I had shared her most intimate confidences, her last thoughts, in which she revealed the rich depths of her beautiful soul. In the beginning I felt a sense of relief; relief that she was out of pain, and that everything she had lived for was now totally fulfilled in another and far happier world; but this relief was short-lived. Like a red hot poker between the eyes, the reality that she was gone for ever kept striking me with blinding force; she who for twenty-six years had given everything to me was dead, and death, I knew, was the end of our life together as we had known it on this earth.

From a little drawer in the bedside table I took out my favourite picture of her, a simple snapshot taken in 1944, just before we were married. She is sitting on the cross-bar of a bicycle, which is resting against a wall, her head bent slightly, her magic eyes looking out and upwards, a gentle friendly smile on her lips. This unpretentious snapshot personifies all that she was, the girl I knew, the girl I fell so hopelessly in love with, the future mother of my children, the woman who unconditionally dedicated her entire short life to me and to all that I was striving for, and trying to achieve.

And as I sat there beside her bed, in the lonely deserted room, holding her crumpled dressing-gown on my knees, the little snapshot in my hands, my memory jumped across the long years to the beginning of my life with Mary.

I first saw her at a dance, on August 5th 1944.

I was a Captain in the Irish Army and I was stationed at Lahinch, on the wild and rugged coast of Clare, where we ran a summer camp for members of the Local Defence Force. These young volunteers sacrificed a lot of free time during the winter months in their home areas, and the army ran summer camps where as much social and pleasurable activity as possible was combined with a week's elementary training. It was a small token reward for a winter's hard and frustrating work. Each week a different goup of L.D.F. came in, but the staff, of whom I was one, remained more or less the same throughout the summer.

The camp consisted of a large building surrounded by hundreds of tents laid out in perfect symmetrical order, and this building was the focal point around which the life of the soldiers revolved. It was made up of various offices, stores, kitchens, and a particularly spacious dining hall capable of seating more than 500 men. At night the tables in this dining hall were folded and stored, and it became a merry ballroom where members of the public, as well as young volunteers and their girl friends, could relax and enjoy themselves in an atmosphere of gaiety, dance, and pleasant music.

On that August night I was duty-officer and I had to keep on the move around the camp, inspecting sentries, visiting the kitchen and making the odd call to the hall where the dancers were enjoying themselves. Because I was on duty and armed, I was forbidden to dance, so I had to content myself in chatting idly with those I knew, or just standing alone in a corner, watching the dancers. Standing there that night, I felt an unfamiliar sadness in my heart, even though the dance was lively and gay. Perhaps the sight of so many enjoying the company of each other, spotlighted, more than usual, the isolation and loneliness of my own self.

The band was playing *Lily Marlene,* which had just come to Ireland across the dark chasm of war. Lonely German soldiers, far from home and from those they loved, sang it nightly in their trenches. British soldiers picked it up on their radios, and its haunting melody expressed for them, too, their deep loneliness and longings. They translated it and made it their own, and in this sentimental little song, with no pretensions to great art, the spirit of the ordinary man, German or English, transcended the hatred and viciousness of the politicians who were hurling these human beings to destruction and death.

I remember the singer who accompanied the band had a husky voice and sang each alternate verse in German and in English, as the couples danced:

Vor der Kaserne, vor dem grossen Tor,
Steht eine Laterne, und steht sie noch davor,
Da wollen wir uns wiederseh'n,
Bei der Laterne woll'n wir steh'n
Wie einst Lily Marlene,
Wie einst Lily Marlene.

It was coming up to midnight and I was about to leave the hall, make out my reports, and go to bed, when my practised eye caught sight a young girl of bewitching beauty, her dark hair hanging loosely over her shoulders, the pale, almost sallow, face of a child, dancing in an uninvolved kind of a way with a young soldier. I stopped dead, as if some invisible magnetic wave had flashed between us. She stopped too, for a split second, and then continued dancing. Something in me gave way and I felt odd and queer and awkward. I was unaccountably nervous and tense and I had lost that suave control I practised when dealing with the opposite sex. I had never felt that way so quickly before, and if anyone present in the hall could have seen into my mind, they would have thought me ludicrous and insane.

My eyes followed her as she danced around and around the hall. I was captivated by her refined beauty, her unusual dignified and graceful form, by a delicate, soft-hued kind of radiance which seemed to envelop her face. I wanted to meet her, to talk to her, to dance with her, to come closer to her. But there was nothing I could do; I was on duty and was prohibited from dancing, and I had no excuse to make contact with her. So I just stood there, astounded at myself, unable to believe that it was I—I who had so often picked up girls at these dances, told them that I loved them, promised them the world, flirted a bit, and then dropped them—and here I was enmeshed in a strange and bewildering emotion that came upon me suddenly and without warning. I knew instinctively that this girl was no pick-up to be played with and then discarded. I was later to find out that behind her soft gentle appearance there was a will of steel.

For no intelligent reason I began to feel jealous that some other man would take her before I had even a chance to speak to her, but when the last dance was called I saw that my fears were groundless. She had no male escort to see her home, and together with a few other girls, she got her coat and left the hall as the band was playing *Lily Marlene* once more, and the husky voice sang the words in English:

Underneath the lamp light by the barrack gate,
Darling, I remember the way you used to wait,

Twas there that you whispered tenderly,
That you loved me, you'd always be
My Lily of the lamp light,
My own Lily Marlene.

That night I slept uneasily, tossing and turning, my mind in turmoil and confusion, and no matter how I tried to reason with myself, to tell myself not to be a fool, that strange mystical face kept haunting me and not letting me rest. Intellectually I knew that the whole situation was absurd, but despite my self-assurance, I had yet to learn that there are forces in life far more powerful than those of the intellect. I was really only beginning to experience my first baptism of fire on the battle-field of complex human emotions.

I imagine that in the lives of every one of us there comes a moment when destiny calls, a moment when eternity is born. In a calmer mood I now began to wonder had the right moment come to me. Was Shakespeare's 'tide in the affairs of men' turning, and just beginning to flood? I was then twenty-eight years old. Like most young army officers I had my share of frivolity and pleasure, and had reached the point where I was beginning to realise that there was something more to life than mere indulgence; I was becoming aware of my own separateness and experiencing a longing for some form of permanent identity. I came into the world without my consent and I would leave it without my consent, and this thought alone gave me a feeling of helplessness, a sense of being trapped, a perception of isolation. I felt I wanted to break through my own loneliness and, above all, reach out to somebody who really cared; I wanted, too, to get above my life, to step into something great, something enduring, and I wanted a kindred soul to share all that with me. Could it be possible that this pale, brown-eyed child was the one? I had not even spoken to her and I knew nothing about her. Some vague, impersonal, sixth sense told me that my search might be over, but I was now absolutely determined to find out.

Days passed and I did not see her again but I was relentless in my search for her. The troops usually trained on the sandhills near the seashore, but there were so many sections, and they were so separated, that it was only possible to supervise them with field glasses; I am afraid I neglected the troops and trained my glasses more often on the sandy beaches where the holiday-makers were swimming and sunbathing. Hour after hour I focused on every nook and cranny, but I never found her. In the evenings I walked and walked the streets of the little village, the promenade, the strand, but she was nowhere to be seen. I was angry with myself in a contradictory kind of a way: on the one hand angry that this young girl had pierced right through all my male defences, and, on the other hand, angry that I could not find her anywhere. Could she have been just a holiday-maker gone home? Had I lost her? Were my dreams of destiny all an illusion?

Then one day a message came to the camp that some wreckage was washed ashore near Quilty, which was about ten miles away, and together with two other officers, I took out the car to drive there and examine what had been washed up. A girl friend of one of the officers lived in Miltown Malbay, which was on our way to Quilty; she was spending a holiday in Lahinch and he thought she might like to drop home for a short visit. Halfway through the village I drove the car into the kerb, while the officer crossed the road to collect his girl. Just as he left, I opened the window and my heart almost stopped. There she was, sitting on a seat outside a guest house, and quite close, as beautiful as when I first saw her. For a moment I was confused and I did not know what to do, but quickly my old military experience with girls stood to me.

I called her over to the car and pretended that I did not know my way to Quilty. She gave me quite detailed instructions how to get there, all of which I deliberately misunderstood, and when I asked questions to which she had already given the answers, she looked at me in a rather puzzled pitying kind of way, as a teacher might look at the classroom dunce. In the end, when I had played out my feigned stupidity, I suggested that she come with us and show us the way. She refused point blank. I was still trying to persuade her when the officer returned with his girl friend. This girl friend knew her, greeted her and told her to sit in, that everything would be all right and that, despite appearances, we were a decent lot of fellows. She thought for a moment and then, seemingly reassured, sat in the back of the car with the other girl. I was delighted; I felt I had won the first round. Just as we were leaving Lahinch village she began to explain the way to Quilty. The other girl burst out laughing and said: 'For heaven's sake, Mary, have sense. They know the way to Quilty well; Sean just used this as an excuse to get you into the car.'

She was silent for a moment. She then put her hand up to her head, brushed the hair from her forehead, and said: 'My God, what a fool I am. I should have known he could not have been as stupid as he pretended.'

'Don't worry,' I answered. 'We will not be longer than an hour and nothing will happen to you.'

We drove the short journey to Quilty and found the wreckage, which was a battered ship's lifeboat, and we had to search around the seashore for scattered fragments. During this time I managed to be alone with her as much as possible, although she took good care to remain near to the others. At close quarters her beauty was striking. Her features were ever so slightly oriental: dark brown eyes set in a sallow face of soft tender skin; black hair hanging loosely over her shoulders; a gracefulness of carriage and bearing; a soft modulated voice with a west of Ireland accent, a remoteness that gave one a strange yet sublime sense of other-worldliness. Throughout her life, this was something even strangers constantly noticed and found hard to explain. I learned her name was Mary Kissane, that she was from Ennis, that she was teaching as a junior assistant in a country school, that she had come to Lahinch for a short holiday. I may say that she did not volunteer this information; she gave it in answer to my questions. She did not, however, ask me any question herself, or show the slightest interest in me.

When we got back to Lahinch I said to her: 'I suppose you are glad to be back again and out of this car.' She smiled, and answered a trifle unconvincingly: 'I am.'

'Well,' I said, 'we are not all that bad. Perhaps I'll see you again?'

There was a second's delay before she answered.

'Perhaps,' she said shyly, and walked slowly away. I was happy; at least the ice was broken.

I did not see her again for five days; how painfully long those five days were! I tried to reason with myself, to tell myself not to be an idiot, but it was no use. The more I did so, the worse it became. I found myself thinking of her almost every moment of every day. She had completely infiltrated my mind and soul. I even bought a special after-shave lotion and an expensive perfumed hair-oil, so that I could appear more beautiful in her presence, but the only effect this had was to make me the butt of fun of my fellow officers.

I have an analytical mind of kinds, and as far as I could possibly control it, I tried never to suppress an idea or emotion. I let them develop fully and totally, tossed them backwards and forwards, and then either accepted or rejected them. This had the effect of leaving me with few inhibitions or frustrations; they had all come out in the open. I tried now to bring this immediate problem out but it defied every analytical attempt. This girl had cast some kind of a spell over me to which there was no answer in my philosophy. Of course I had been many, many times 'in love'. I had experienced over and over again that wonderful emotional intoxication, that ecstasy which transports a human being from this earth and makes him want to spin the world in the palm of his hand. But what I was experiencing now was very different; it seemed to burn me up as if I were engulfed in a mystical and invisible flame; it penetrated through my whole being. No matter how I tried to bring the principles of philosophy and wisdom to bear upon it, I just failed. I was absent from myself. In the end I gave up, and admitted that I was falling in love with somebody I hardly knew, somebody who had not even tried to attract me; and it would be just my luck if she rejected me.

I met her again at a dance in the hall and, as I was off duty, I successfully managed to dance with her most of the evening, and again she answered all my questions but volunteered little information or comment. I was not, however, without hope. I noticed that, when each new dance was announced, she glanced immediately in my direction, even though I might have been across the hall. Rather nervously, I offered to see her home afterwards; quietly she refused, saying that she had come with some friends and that she was going home with them. I did, however, succeed in getting her to agree to meet me for lunch the following day.

She turned up on time at the Aberdeen Arms Hotel, not alone as I had hoped, but with a girl, Mary Tuttle, whom she introduced as her cousin. It was quite clear she was taking no chances with me. The lunch went off normally. I cannot now recall the conversation; I can only recall that I did most of the talking and they just listened as I spoke with all the arrogance of youth trying to impress a girl. When lunch was over they agreed to my suggestion of a drive along the coast. I opened the front door of the car and let Mary in, and then went to the back door to open it for her cousin. On a wild impulse I paused, turned to her cousin, and said:

'I desperately want to be alone with Mary for a short while, please understand. Everything will be all right. I give you my word on that.'

She smiled in a friendly, trusting kind of way, so I jumped into the driver's seat and drove off without her. Mary did not panic. She remained silent for a few moments, then looked calmly across at me and said:

'This is the second time I have been tricked into going for a drive with you. What do you want?'

'Don't worry,' I said, 'I promise I will never trick you again; I only want to be with you and to talk to you. Please believe me; I am quite sincere.'

We drove along in silence for a short while and I then turned the car down a lonely by-road towards the sea. She now looked frightened, and disturbed.

'Where are you taking me to?' she asked.

'Don't be afraid,' I answered reassuringly. 'There is something important I want to say to you. I promise you, you have nothing to fear.'

On a gravel strand, by the edge of the sea, I parked the car.

'Well,' she said nervously, 'what do you want to say?'

'There is no use beating about the bush,' I answered. 'I am very attracted towards you. I want to know you better. In fact I think I am beginning to fall in love with you.'

I had got it all off my chest in one go, and I felt a great sense of relief. The ball was now in her court. She was silent for a while as she looked out to sea through the open window of the car. It seemed an eternity before she spoke, but when she did, the nervousness was gone.

'I have heard quite a bit about you,' she said calmly. 'You are supposed to be the Don Juan of the army around here. I can name at least three or four girls in Clare whose hopes you raised, only to dash them to the ground again. Do you want to do the same with me?'

How can you parry a question like that, so direct and so sincere? What she had said was true. In her strange, ethereal presence, I could only come straight and clean, and I admitted the truth of everything, but secretly I was overjoyed. I now knew that she cared enough to make enquiries about me.

I suppose that in most of us there are two diametrically opposed personalities, the Dr. Jekyll and Mr. Hyde, the Ariel and Caliban. I had clearly recognised these in myself: on the one hand I could be boisterous, wild and irresponsible; on the other I could be recollected, contemplative and even religious. In between was a façade I put on every day.

Mary had seen the façade and, as one would expect in an Irish setting, she had heard about the unpleasant side of my character first, and I felt fairly sure her informants were not over restrained in the telling. I thought she should see the other side, so I began to tell her about myself and about what I really wanted in life.

I told her of my unhappy childhood, of my early ideals, of my burning desire to do something purposeful with my life. I remember how I spoke at length about my utter disillusionment with the army. I explained the aimlessness and boredom of an Irish officer's life; he could not show any initiative; his work was fettered by hundreds of petty regulations, each made out not in the interests of the army, but to save some civil servant's skin and enable him to put the blame anywhere rather than on himself. An officer who thought for himself and acted accordingly could be doomed. The Irish Army was not an army, but an impotent branch of the civil service. I remember clearly giving her the following example: If a company of 200 men, commanded by a captain, could not march, shoot or fight, nothing would happen to the captain; but if that same company were highly efficient in every branch of military science, yet deficient in a few knives, forks, spoons, or blankets on inspection, the captain in charge could get into serious trouble, could find his promotion blocked, and perhaps lose a considerable amount of salary. The moral, therefore, was to concentrate on the non-essentials, spoons, knives, forks, and forget about training the men to be good soldiers. She was quite surprised to hear all this, and she understood, when I impressed upon her, that whatever happened, I could never devote my life to such utter futility.

I told her of my life-long interest in books, and how I was trying to find a way to express myself through this medium. I explained my ideas for a publishing house as a means of fulfilling my life, and how I had made one tentative experiment with success. Quite by chance I had a letter in my pocket from Dom Eugene Boylan encouraging me in every way to go ahead with the idea of *The Mercier Press*. In my effort to convince her of my sincerity, I handed her the letter to read. She read it slowly and folded it up in her hand. I did not see that letter again until after her death; I found it carefully wrapped in tissue paper, in a little safe where she kept her most personal and intimate possessions.

I talked to her about what I believed love should be. I explained that I thought real love was based on the principle of two bodies and one soul, not two different souls in two different bodies. If two people were really in love, then everything in their lives was negotiable with each other; there were no fixed boundaries or restrictions. Real love, as distinct from selfish love, meant the fusion of two souls into one, and this fusion called for the total destruction of egoism. It also meant that the continued existence of this new soul was one of extreme delicacy, and to survive the trials and crises of life called for personal discipline, sacrifice, loyalty, tolerance, and tenderness. I had seen many lovers start out with one soul, and through selfishness and egoism end up in misery, two separate beings. Instead of playing lovers' games, which I normally did, I spoke openly that which was most intimate in me, and when I ended I was completely astonished at myself. I had never spoken like this to any other person. Now it was I who was nervous and shaking.

'There is nothing more I can tell you,' I said, 'except perhaps to say that my worldly pursuits, and that includes chasing females, may only be a search for life's purpose, in reverse.'

The flood of words was over and I had for the first time unburdened my soul to a stranger.

After a long pause she turned and looked me straight in the eyes.

'A short while ago,' she said, 'you told me you were falling in love with me. Just to how many other girls did you say exactly the same words?'

Dear God! Was my outburst all for nothing? The question put with such utter simplicity and directness pierced every defence. Clearly she was not going to be fooled; she was no naive, credulous school-child.

'You are not the first,' I admitted. 'Not by a long shot. But I am going to say something to you now that I never said to any other girl.' Slowly and deliberately, with dry frightened lips, I heard myself pronouncing the words:

'I want you to marry me!'

Calmly, she turned her head away and looked out to sea.

A few weeks after her death, when the pain of loneliness was tearing me asunder, I was, one day, aimlessly wandering from room to room in the empty house. Suddenly, on a wild impulse, I sat into the car, drove the long journey from Cork to Lahinch, and revisited all those scenes; the hall where I first saw her, the street where we first spoke, the hotel where we lunched. I drove down the lonely by-road to the strand, where I had unburdened my soul to her, and parked the car in the same spot. The agony of it all was so terrible that I thought I had reached the limit of human endurance and I could not imagine that any suffering, either in this world or in the next, could be more painful. I opened the window and looked out to sea, as she had done on that afternoon twenty-six years ago, when I asked her to marry me.

I remembered how she had looked through the open window out to the horizon. In the distance a summer haze covered the Aran Islands. I remembered how the sea broke softly against the shore and the gulls were gliding almost stationary in the sky. The gentle Atlantic breeze had blown the tresses of her dark hair across her face. She kept gazing out to sea, her head turned away from me. After what seemed an age, I remembered breaking the silence.

'Mary, did you hear what I said? I am asking you to marry me.' Then she slowly turned her head towards me. Tears were beginning to flow from her soft, brown eyes. In that moment I knew my search was over, my eternity was born. Tenderly I took her hand in mine and pressed it to my lips.

Three months later we were married.

Chapter Two

When everything around a man is wavering, when the unknown future is dark and featureless, when the whole world of ideas vanishes in smoke and all things are penetrated with doubt, the faithful heart of a woman is the only fixed point which may still be his. There he may rest his head. There he will find the strength to live, the strength to believe, and if need be the strength to die.

Amiel

One of the terrible things about the death of someone you love is that life must go on, and it goes on relentlessly. The morning Mary died the postman came as usual. He delivered two letters: one was a final demand for Income Tax; the other a brochure suggesting a holiday for two on the Riviera. The milkman rattled the bottles as he delivered the milk. The daily papers were dropped in the letterbox. Cars and buses drove up and down the main road. Planes zoomed overhead. The life of the city went on as if nothing had happened. But something *had* happened. Mary had just died. I worked myself into a senseless anger because everything continued as if she were still alive; life ignored her death as if it were a thing of nothing. I wanted to rush out on to the streets, halt the traffic, and shout on the top of my voice to everyone to stop—to shout in the loudest voice that Mary was dead and that the world was at an end.

This, of course, was a temporary, if understandable, insanity. The world was not at an end; only my world seemed to be and that, too, would change. The world at large did not really care one damn whether Mary was dead or alive, and bitter though this thought was, I had to accept it. I even knew that when those now passing the door so indifferently had died, others would pass their doors indifferently, and go on their way with scarcely a thought. Individuals live, suffer, die, and are forgotten; the herd goes callously on, without pity, without compassion, without remorse. This is the unchangeable, immutable law of life from which there is no escape, and the sooner I tried to come to terms with it the better.

One of the painful things I had to do that morning was to arrange for the opening of our grave in Dualla, a small village near Cashel in the County Tipperary, some sixty miles from Cork. I was born nearby and lived there almost all my early life. When I was five years old my mother, who taught in Dualla school, died; ten months before that, my brother Gerald, died too. Both were buried together in Dualla graveyard. This was the spot chosen by Mary as her last resting place.

It is a peaceful little country churchyard, surrounded by hills, on the edge of the Golden Vale. Tall trees line the roadside and the querulous voices of the nesting crows remind one harshly of the fleetness of life. A week before we were married, Mary and I visited Dualla. It was her first time there, and she seemed to have fallen in love at once with the simple little country graveyard.

'If I die before you,' she said reflectively, 'I want to be buried here.' As we strolled around and about the graves, I 'introduced' her to all the dead. They were old friends of mine. I had shared their world and we had lived in the shadow of one another. Like most, they had their faults, but their virtues outshone them. Maybe if a drop of drink was going the rounds it went to their heads all too quickly, and then there was laughter and song and story, and sometimes the odd fight, for as long as the drop lasted. They were a simple, proud people, Irish through and through, who had accepted life with its joys and sorrows, and who had faced death, when it came, with calmness and courage.

We lingered a little to read the beautiful inscription in Irish over the graves of Pierce McCann, T.D., the Hogans, the Loobys, and Delaneys, who had so bravely given their lives for the ideals they believed in, and whose bullet-ridden bodies rested side by side with those for whom they died.

'This is surely the place for me,' she said almost with enthusiasm. 'Here, with your mother, and with all those whom I now regard as my friends, too.'

As we stood in silence over our family grave, Mary impulsively asked me to recite Sir William Butler's poem, *A Request.* Since our engagement, we had had many poetry-reading sessions together, during which I had recited, among others, this beautiful poem, which was so apt in the rural surroundings of Dualla. Sometimes now, when I stand over her grave, alone and lonely, I find myself reciting the poem in a low voice, as I did that day, so many years ago:

Give me but six foot three (one inch to spare)
Of Irish earth, and dig it anywhere;
And for my poor soul say an Irish prayer
Above the spot.
Let it be where cloud and hillside meet,
Or vale where grows the tufted meadow sweet
Or boreen trod by peasants shoeless feet;
It matters not.

I loved them all—the vale, the hill,
The moaning sea, the water-lilied rill.
The yellow gorse, the lake shore lone and still
The wild birds song.
But more than hill or valley, bird or moor,
More than the green fields of the river Suir
I loved those hapless ones, the Irish poor,
All my life long.
So give me Irish grave, mid Irish air
With Irish grass above it everywhere
And let some Irish peasant say a prayer
For my soul's sake.

We were young then, and it was easy to recite poetry and to talk about death. As we walked arm in arm together through the graveyard, death, although all around, seemed so remote and far away; only life counted then, our life together, which was blossoming out in the fresh springtime of our young love. For us it was the morning of the world.

But Dualla remained in Mary's mind, and she did not let me forget it. Every year we went there, once or perhaps twice, to clean and tidy the grave, to bring flowers, and to pray in the old and tired church.

I remember well, so well, our last visit. It was in October 1970, just a few months before she died. The autumn wind was gently blowing the brown leaves as they glided slowly and reluctantly from the trees. She was in such pain that she could only walk by clinging on to me with one hand and heavily leaning on a strong walking stick with the other. She was unusually silent as she painfully limped her way to the grave which was to receive her all too soon. She stood with her head down, just looking at the brown earth. Inside the church, instead of kneeling and praying, we stayed near the door and gazed reflectively towards the altar. All was silent except for the ticking of the old clock on the wall. She must have known that the end was very near, and I did not intrude on her thoughts. One senses those unfathomable moments in human life, those moments that are too pregnant with meaning to disturb with the slightest sound; and this was one of them. After a shorter stay than usual we slowly made our way, bit by bit, back to the car. As we were leaving the graveyard, she turned around and looked rather strangely at the grave for a long time. Did she know the next time it would be for ever? As I was helping her into the car, I sensed she was fighting desperately to hold back the tears.

We drove slowly and silently along in the Autumn sunshine. A short distance from the graveyard we parked the car, sat on a roadside fence and began to partake of our sandwiches and tea. It was October at its very best. Everywhere was full of colour, rich and splendid. The dew had not completely evaporated, and the threads of gossamer were still glistening in the tall grass. The leaves were dropping ever so slowly from the trees. In the bitter-sweetness of this Autumn day, it seemed as if we were eavesdropping on the last moments of a dying beauty. Again Mary was unusually silent. I imagine that in the peaceful stillness we were both afraid to express the sad heavy thoughts which undoubtedly filled our minds. In my heart there was a gloomy emptiness.

In the distance a postman came cycling along the narrow leaf-covered road, his bicycle creaking in the silence. When he reached us he dismounted. He was Pat Kirwan, an old friend of ours, and we chatted together, the three of us, about all the recent happenings in the locality, who was born, who married, who died. Unaware, he poignantly mentioned two women who had died from cancer. Mary showed no sign of emotion. He was on his rounds and could not stay too long, and as he was remounting his bicycle he said:

'I am glad you are both looking so well. I hope we will see each other soon again.'

The next time I saw him, a few months later, was at Mary's open grave, for it was to Pat I turned the morning of her death, for help, and like the true friend he is, he dropped everything and set about the task of digging her grave. There are no professional grave-diggers in Dualla. This sad charge is willingly carried out by kind and sympathetic friends. Pat collected three companions of my youth, Philip Bulfin, Paddy and Tony Higgins, and together they dug and opened Mary's grave. Sparsely scattered through the brown earth they found the remnants of my mother's bones. With reverent care they assembled and reburied them in a spot which would be just under Mary's coffin. The mortal remains of the two women closest to me in life would now rest together until the end of time.

*

Dearest Mary: As I write these lines in the early hours of a cold Spring morning, you are almost a year dead. Outside dawn is breaking, and I can hear the first musical notes of the birds. Far away in Dualla I am sure they are singing too. I am slowly adjusting myself to life without your physical presence. I spend a lot of time now in the Dublin office, and I have a little flat all to myself in a quiet tree-lined avenue in the suburbs. Most of my week-ends I spend at Longfield House, Cashel, where Christa and Kevin Byrne look after me as if I were their closest friend. They have given me a beautiful semi-circular room at the top of the house with a magnificent view across the valley of the Suir. I can almost see the house where I was born, with Dualla graveyard just beyond in the trees. I am able to visit your grave every Sunday and I always manage, even in winter, to get a few flowers which I lay against the Celtic cross over it. Soon the new church will be finished and the main altar will be dedicated to your memory. But all these things, however touching, cannot help. You are gone and they cannot bring you back.

The scenery in and around Longfield has a beauty all its own, a beauty you would love. Sometimes at night I wander about the soft moonlit fields, and I sense you so very close that I can almost feel the touch of your hand. I walk alone through the meadows and the woods and the river bank, and you are always in my mind, always with me. In the early morning I watch the sun rising and the dawn creeping over the mountains, and I wonder if you are there, behind it, coming with it. When the glorious day comes across the fields and hedgerows, and the clouds are making all kinds of magic shapes against the blue sky, I wonder if you are hiding behind one and looking down at me. I see you sketched on a transparent canvas softly and mysteriously across the earth as the whitethorn bursts like foam over the land. The dignity of your beauty is reflected everywhere in nature; I hear your voice in the sounds of the earth and the singing of the birds. Every wayside flower smiles your smile; for every tree and every flower is eternal life. . . . But you are gone and all I have is memories . . . memories which inspire me, not with despair, but with courage and hope . . .

*

Our short engagement gave us very little time to prepare for the material side of our life. Mary was then twenty years old and I was twenty-eight. We faced all our problems full of hope and with that glorious impulsiveness of youth. After a long search we managed to rent a delightful flat overlooking the river Lee, at what then appeared to be the extravagent rent of £1 per week. The flat was unfurnished and new furniture was hard to get because the war was still on and everything was in short supply. We had little money, so I sold my car for £100 and used this to buy second-hand furniture at the various weekly auctions, but despite this shortage of money, I managed to buy her an engagement ring with three diamonds for £27, and a wedding ring for £5. These rings were the symbols of our total commitment to each other, of our belief and hope in the future.

In the last week of her life, as she lay unconscious on her death-bed, I held her wasted hand in mine for hours on end, gently fondling those rings with which we began our life together, and I realised how she, in her life, had fulfilled everything they symbolised, where I had so hopelessly failed. When, after her death, I put her wedding ring on my own finger, I prayed that with it might come some of her courage, her greatness to inspire me to fulfil many of the ideals I failed to fulfil while she was still alive.

In those weeks after her death, when I was painfully going through her belongings, I found a small fire-proof safe which I managed to open with difficulty. It contained a mass of letters, almost every one that I had ever written, from the time I met her until the end of her life. Those early letters make strange reading now, and hardly any one of them would find a place in an anthology of great love letters. Here is an extract from one written just before we were married:

> The flat is in fair shape now. I have two 4′ beds complete with mattresses, sheets, blankets, eiderdowns, a very large three part mahogany wardrobe, a chest of drawers and a bedside table. In the sitting room I have two armchairs newly covered, a large oak dining table, four mahogany dining chairs with

seats of red plush, a small side table and a small book case. I am arranging to get a dust-bin and a turf container. All that is really required now are kitchen utensils, table cloths and curtains.

And so we began our married life, with little of the world's goods, but what we had were paid for and we had no debts. We were five years married before we got our first electric cooker, eight years before our first refrigerator, and ten years before we could afford a car. But when we got these items, they were our own, and we had an easy mind.

The pattern of married life which I had seen, and which I read about in books and newspapers, did not exactly coincide with what I now began to experience. I was under the impression that the first years would be appallingly difficult, as most of my friends said so, and I expected all kinds of fights and rows where two strange personalities were trying to adjust to each other. I had for various short periods of my life lived with young married couples, who never seemed to stop fighting and squabbling. I was also familiar with the many Army officers who, on occasions, slept for a few nights in barracks, and who were good-humouredly referred to as suffering from 'wife trouble'; and sometimes in their cups they would reveal a frightening picture of married life. This was what I had known, but I was not really sure what to expect. Would it happen to me? Would I be one of those sleeping regularly in barracks? Time proved my fears groundless. We had, of course, our disagreements, but they were few and we forgot about them quickly, and there were no long periods of sulking in silence, which are such fertile breeding grounds for real hatred. It was a kind of a coincidence that we both approached marriage with much the same outlook. From the start we seemed to have got off to a very mature love, a union in which each of us preserved our individuality while being completely united. We both started with the fundamental belief that the success of any human relationship depended entirely on the individual approaching it from the point of view of what can be *given,* not what one can *get.* The *get* part follows naturally on the *give,* but it is inferior to it. I was determined that everything I could give Mary would be given, and this did not just mean material things: it meant time, patience, tolerance, and above all good humour. I am afraid I did not always succeed, but I tried hard.

Mary responded to my feeble attempts a hundredfold and, by creating a beautiful home and an uncomplicated life, she made it possible for me to make a success of my work. She saw that in starting and promoting *The Mercier Press* I had a task above the ordinary, and she quickly realised that every day brought new problems, new difficulties; she made life at home run as easily and smoothly as possible, so that when I came home in the evenings, tired and weary, like a wounded soldier, there awaited me a tastefully cooked meal, a glowing fire, an understanding wife who made the home a place of rest and repose. If there were problems to be solved, she deferred them until late evening, and she only brought them forward when I specifically enquired. She was not one who said: 'I want this, I want that, I must go out so many times a week, I must have these clothes or that holiday.' Demanding, so commonplace in many women, was not in her nature. Neither did she try to change me or my ways; she accepted me as I was, with all my complications and idiosyncrasies. She disagreed with a lot I said and did, but she rarely made an issue of it, and when I had made a fool of myself, and she knew it, and I knew it, there were no recriminations. Whatever she may have felt deep down in her heart at what I did, she was never disloyal to me, and never ran to others with complaints. She believed that one can only influence by love and not by force, moods or tantrums; and that love, which expressed itself on every level of living, she gave without stinting.

Perhaps what struck me most about her in those early months of marriage was her mature outlook. It was only after many years I came to realise, that maturity is one of the really great virtues a woman can have. She was calm, dignified in all situations, with almost complete control over her temper; she thought long and hard before she made an important decision, but once it was made she would not easily change, however emotionally charged the appeal was. She was in direct contrast to so many women who seemed to have a kind of a grass-hopper mind, and who in a matter of hours could do a complete about face, change important and far-reaching decisions, and then change them back again with the next emotional wind. This firmness of purpose led to those who came in close contact with her having a complete and absolute trust; and she was then just turned twenty years of age.

Because of my long standing wish for a life with more purpose and fulfilment than the Army could offer, I had been making my first tentative experiments in the world of literature. In my book *An Irish Publisher and His World*, I have told the story of the founding and early years of *The Mercier Press,* and in 1945 I came a step nearer to my goal when, together with J. C. O'Connor, and Mary, a limited company was formed and we began publishing in real earnest. But before this there were months of preparations which Mary shared fully with me: manuscripts had to be read and prepared for press, proofs corrected, jackets designed, a catalogue compiled. Mary took care of all this work, which was carried out mostly in our flat, working long hours into the night. She was our first editor, proof-reader, accountant, etc., and one of the three first directors. She remained a director until she died.

As the years passed *The Mercier Press* grew slowly from

strength to strength, and the inevitable day arrived when it was no longer possible to remain a part-time publisher. I had now to make a major decision which would not only affect my own life, but would affect Mary's as well. Would I stay in the Army, secure, well-paid, pensionable; or would I leave, and put our lives at the mercy of the hazardous world of publishing, which could at any moment crash and leave us penniless? For years I had longed for the day when I could shake off the uniform and begin what I thought was my real life, but now that the moment had arrived, I found myself, to say the least, cowardly and afraid. In leaving the last word to Mary, I was half hoping that she would choose security, and for the rest of my days I could have the excuse that I had to give priority to the wishes of my wife. But, as so often happened, I completely underestimated her.

'You must find fulfilment in your life so that you realise your own self and do the work you really want to,' she said quietly. 'Leave the Army. We'll work hard, and having done that, put our trust in God.'

'But it might fail,' I argued. 'And we could starve.'

'If that happens,' she answered, 'we'll starve together.' And then she added with a whimsical smile: 'Don't you think that the risks I took in marrying you were greater than the risks here and now? Despite your complicated personality, you have the ability to succeed and you will. If you, with your great energies, put your mind to anything you cannot fail.'

And so, with an almost sinking heart, I left the world of security and turned my face to the unknown. In the economic insecurity of those early years, Mary was never afraid, and she had unbounded confidence in my ability to make a success of what I was doing. This silent trust drove me on and on to try to achieve more and more for her sake.

As time went by and *The Mercier Press* kept growing,

separation became part and parcel of our lives, as I had to travel abroad a great deal, and this meant long absences at a time. The children were young and had to be looked after, so she stayed at home. She was not a great admirer of the travelling wife, and she believed that wives who insisted on going everywhere with their husbands were suffering from some deep-seated emotional insecurity. Nevertheless, I know she was human and would have liked to come with me, but she put her wishes and desires in the background when she felt that the better fulfilment of my work was in question. She was the most truly and completely unselfish person I ever knew. In a small way I tried to ease her loneliness by writing to her almost every day. It was only when she was dead, and when I opened her little safe, that I fully realised how much she cherished these notes so hastily and carelessly written. She had kept them all, hundreds of them, postcards and letters which I sent her from all parts of the world.

Another aspect of my work in *The Mercier Press* was entertaining the frequent visitors, associated with writing and publishing, who came to Cork. They were mainly writers, journalists, foreign publishers, broadcasters, or public figures of some kind. Cork is a moderately sized city and we tried to make those who visited the firm feel as much at home as possible, and this usually meant taking them out to dinner at night and not leaving them to themselves. Here again Mary showed her wonderful unselfishness and good taste. She believed that it was not her place to attend these dinners where technical and other matters were being discussed. She felt, rather, that I and other members of the permanent staff were best left alone with these visitors. She did, however, suggest that I bring them out to the house afterwards for a final nightcap, and in this way she met and got to know the famous and the great, and indeed sometimes the infamous and the superficial. In this company, she kept quietly in the background, saw that everyone's needs were looked after, and in her own unique way created an atmosphere of personal friendship which was given to all. After her death, the constant recurring theme in so many letters and expressions or sympathy was: 'I only met her once but there was something about her which made a lasting impression on me.' And what an unusual medley of people came to the house over the years; cardinals, bishops, generals, cabinet ministers, singers, actors, painters—you name it—they were there. And what was to be a short nightcap, more often than not, ended only with the dawn.

The morning she died a taxi pulled up at the door and the driver delivered a letter addressed to me. I found it hard to keep emotionally steady as I read the following lines:

> What I admired most in Mary was her serenity and the sense of goodness she radiated. I figured her values were the right ones and that is why her good opinion meant a lot to me. I felt that if I were all right in her books a lot of nasty things people said about me were probably not true.
>
> I remember her so well the night Sarah Churchill and her party were at your house. She was taking in the atmosphere of the company with silent pleasure, eyes dancing, but remaining in the background to see that everything ran perfectly. That is how she was for me.

The letter was signed: Ulick O'Connor.

Our four children came into the world in quick succession. Kathleen came first; she is now married and teaching in Cork. Gerald was second; he is a chef in a Dublin hotel. Sean was third; he is an Antiquarian bookseller and runs the shop in Bridge Street which his mother started for him. Mary, the youngest, having taken her degrees in the University, is editor of *The Mercier Press*.

Mary's pregnancies were normal and without complications. She was by any standards a strikingly beautiful woman and, like most really beautiful women, she did not think of herself that way. She seemed to reach the highest point of her beauty when she was pregnant. Her whole face took on a radiance that was indescribable; she seemed to have been enveloped in Beauty itself, and I watched this, with awe and admiration, during each of her four pregnancies. I saw it once again, for the last time, when she lay in her coffin.

When the children reached a more manageable age, and when we could afford it, we did go abroad together, not on business, but on holiday: to France, Germany, Holland, Spain, and once to the U.S.A. Of all the places we visited, the one which she liked most, and to which she returned again and again, was Lourdes. She paid little heed to the miracles and rather treated them with scepticism, but she saw in the life of Bernadette not the visions and revelations, but the long road of physical pain that Bernadette trod, and that she herself was destined to follow. When it was night and everyone had left the grotto she would sit there alone, just thinking. Did she have premonitions of the suffering to come? Did the spirit of Bernadette, shorn of the empty trappings, inspire her with the courage and fortitude to face her terrible destiny. Only to herself, and to God, are these things known. She never spoke of them.

During the first fifteen years of our married life, there was absolutely no reason to suspect that she had any tendency to cancer. This, of course, did not mean very much, since the causes and origin of cancer are unknown. Her health could be described as good, if not excellent. There were a few unusual aspects to which, perhaps, we did not pay enough attention at the time. Illnesses such as diphtheria and measles, which normally come once in a lifetime, she got twice. She also had a tendency to change weight rapidly, so that clothes which would fit her one day might be either too large or too small a few days later. Here, I believe, we should have paused and had her examined thoroughly, and this examination might have given us a clue. She was herself concerned about her heart, which sometimes beat very irregularly, and occasionally she suffered from great shortness of breath. She was prone to most common ailments, colds, 'flus, infections; if they were around, she got them. But on the whole there was never any real cause for alarm, and there was not the slightest reason to suspect that she would not attain a normal old age.

We often talked about our old age together, where we would retire to and what we would do. I was fairly sure that I would die long before her, and indeed I had arranged all my material affairs on this assumption although, on the other hand, she never seemed to be entirely convinced that she would live to be very old. She once said to me that she thought it was easier to die than to grow old; that death is one final act of destruction, while growing old is a series of smaller decays that gnaw away at our lives day by day. Almost in the same breath she said: 'The great argument against marriage is that one partner must die first and leave the other in pain.'

But all these gloomy things were far away below the horizon, and we did not see them or even think they were there. Life was full for us then and we enjoyed, as far as our limited resources allowed, the good things: travel, music, reading, good friends, social outings and very occasionally a dinner-dance.

I have good reason to remember one of these dinner-dances in 1960; the function was run by the Rotary Club of Cork. It was an evening of gaiety, laughter, merriment, and good cheer, despite the cultivated deceit and emptiness one sees in most faces at these parties. The dance was in full swing, the music soft and clear, the spotlights whirling in multi-colours on the walls and ceilings; it was like fairyland. I thought she was a little more silent than usual and somewhat out of sorts, so once or twice I asked her if anything were wrong, but she parried my questions. When the dance was over, a few friends came to our home for a nightcap. Mary was not her usual self, and I began to examine my conscience to see if I had done something to offend her, but I could not recall anything. When everyone had gone, I again asked her if anything were wrong. She was sitting in an armchair, gazing into the fire. Only the ticking of the grandfather clock broke the silence. Hoppy, her favourite dog, was sitting on her knee. Quietly and serenely she answered:

'I have found two small lumps on my breast. I think it could be cancer.'

She was then thirty-four years of age.

Chapter Three

The beautiful souls of this world have an art of saintly alchemy by which bitterness is converted into kindness; the gall of human experience into gentleness; ingratitude into goodness; insults into pardon. The transformation is so easy that lookers-on think it spontaneous.

Amiel

In spite of the comings and goings of relatives and friends, the bustle and activity of the day, I knew that the most dreaded and most painful moment of all was drawing nearer and nearer. How would I react when I saw Mary dead? What would I feel when I gazed on her lifeless body and realised that never again would I hear her soft voice, look into her gentle brown eyes, stroke her dark, luxuriant hair untouched by grey? Would I break down helplessly like a child, or could I hold myself together with courage and dignity? Often over the past four years I thought about it; I even once talked it over with her. She had asked me straight out how I would react when I saw her dead, and I told her that, if possible, I would not look at her at all; that I would prefer to remember her as she was, alive, beautiful and well. But now that the moment had arrived, I knew this attitude was unthinkable, and despite the feeling of fear and terror churning up inside me, I wanted to see her in death, wanted to say a last good-bye.

At six-thirty in the evening two limousines arrived at the house to take us to St. Patrick's Hospital. The four children and myself travelled in one; her sister Eily, her brothers Pat and Sean in the other. The main rush-hour traffic was over and, as we sped towards the city, I impulsively asked the driver to go slowly, saying that I did not want to arrive at the hospital too early. The moment I had spoken, I knew that I was wrong, and I knew my words were the first sign of a cowardly panic. My heart beat wildly. What could I do to control myself? It was too late to take a sedative, or even a drink. After a few moments of near-hysteria, I thought of the greatness, the nobility, the bravery that was Mary. And then I did a strange thing; I prayed to her, not aloud, but in my heart: *Dear Mary, I feel I am going to pieces. Do not let me. Hold me together at least until I get home again. I beg you guide me through the next few hours so that I may act and conduct myself in a way you can be proud of.* It was crude; it was cowardly; it was a last cry from the depth of despair. But it worked...

When we arrived at the hospital, I stepped out of the car and, together with the children, walked calmly up the steps and down the corridor to the little oratory where she lay in her coffin. The place was crowded with friends and sympathisers. Two nuns were reciting the rosary aloud, and the crowd was responding.

I stood directly over the coffin and looked down. There she lay, in all the icy beauty of death. Her body was enfolded in her blue Child of Mary cloak; her face delicately covered with a white transparent veil; her hands joined together in prayer; a rosary beads of Connemara marble entwined through her waxen fingers. This was Mary, the woman I loved, the woman who was my life, now cold and dead. But her face was no longer torn by pain and suffering; it was the face of a child, striking in its beauty and serenity, like the face of a Renaissance madonna.

A smile of triumph was on her lips. I was now no longer out of control; she was watching over me, as she had promised. I was uplifted at the thought that that part of her which was eternal, which had given us so much happiness, had gone to a new life, a life where there was no more sadness, or suffering, or disillusionment, or death. She knew the answers to all the perplexing questions which have baffled mankind since the dawn of time. The Book of Life was no longer closed. She saw the totality of Truth, experienced the boundless joy of Goodness, and was surely reposing in a Beauty without end. Her victory was now complete.

In the shadowy candlelight of the little oratory, a priest began to recite the prayers for the dead. I should have prayed with him, but in the anguish and torture of my heart, I could not pray; instead, the words of a beautiful poem by Coventry Patmore, expressing his sorrow when confronted with the dead body of the woman he loved, flashed across my mind. Sadly he reproached her for leaving him; I, too, wanted to reproach Mary, sadly, for having left me:

It was not like your great and gracious ways!
Do you that have naught other to lament,
Never, my love, repent
Of how that afternoon
You went
With sudden unintelligible phrase
And frightened eye,
Upon your journey of so many days
Without a single kiss or a good-bye . . .

But she was gone; and nothing on this earth, neither philosophy, nor poetry, nor prayers, nor tears, could bring her back.

Before they put the lid on the coffin, I bent down and tenderly kissed her cold lips, and I knew that this moment of terrible beauty would be embedded in my memory, and would remain there all the days of my life.

I no longer remember the short journey from the hospital to the church, but vaguely I recall the hearse and a long stream of cars. Inside the church they rested her coffin on a catafalque, surrounded by four lighted candles. Wreaths of multi-coloured flowers lined the walls and covered the coffin itself. In the dim light of the church, the rosary was said and the crowd began to leave one by one. Outside I can only recall a sea of faces, faces of strangers, faces of friends, some of whom I had not seen for years; they came in twos and threes, shaking my hand, all expressing their sorrow. Mary and I had done the same, so many times, at the funerals of our friends. Now it was her turn. One day, too, it would be mine. Through the crowd I made my way back to the car where the children were waiting, and we drove home.

That night, just as I had gone to bed, young Mary handed me a packet. It was from the hospital, and inside I found her rings, which the nun had taken from her lifeless finger, and a large tress of her dark flowing hair.

Impulsively I pressed her hair to my lips. All my defences collapsed and I burst out crying. I cried as I never remember having cried before.

*

Mary dear: I should not have cried that night. I am supposed to be a man of strength and maturity, but everything within me went to pieces, and I became just a whimpering child, although I was consoled by remembering Victor Frankel's words that there was no need to be ashamed of tears, for tears bore witness that a man had the greatest of courage, the courage to suffer. I lay in your bed with all the memories of those last harrowing days around me, and I could only see your beautiful face immobile in death. This vision has never left me. I see it last thing before I sleep at night and first thing when I awake at dawn. I see it as I walk the streets of the city, or drive through the beautiful countryside, or sail the stormy seas. It comes between me and all created things. But it is not a morbid vision. It is pregnant with inspiration. Sometimes when life deals out one of those cruel blows which sends me reeling to the ground with such force that I can hardly arise, I see your godlike face, as I last saw it in the coffin, and it inspires me with the courage to rise once more and to go right on. It makes me realise that, in some mysterious way, you are always with me, always by my side, not just helping me, but what is far more important, making me help myself. And sometimes in these unpleasant moments, I recall how you yourself, when things looked their blackest, used to smile happily, put your arm in mine and quote aloud Browning's brave and immortal words:

Then welcome each rebuff
That turns earth's smoothness rough,
Each sting that bids nor sit nor stand but go;
Be our joys three parts pain;
Strive and hold cheap the strain;
Learn, nor account the pang; dare never grudge the throe.

★

Cancer is not a new disease; indeed it is a very old one. In the year 430 B.C., the great historian Herodotus wrote of the Queen of Persia:

> Atossa had a growth on her breast which was ulcerated and spreading. While the lump had been small she had been too modest to show it to anyone. Now, since it had become worse, she consulted Democedes.

He further records that Atossa was temporarily cured, but it looks as if her chances of a long life were slim. Cancer has attacked and killed mankind down the centuries and, despite the heroic and persistent efforts of dedicated scientists and doctors, it has so far eluded all remedy. Why should a group of cells multiply and career wildly into shapeless masses destroying all before them, including life itself? Why should mankind's greatest brains have failed to find a cure? The answers to these terrible questions remain as yet unknown. Everything so far has been just hit or miss; and it has been mostly miss. Today the word 'cancer' is almost synonomous with the word 'death'.

But there is some slight ray of hope in this picture of gloom. If cancer is detected early and eradicated in time, human life has a fair chance of being saved; the problem is to detect it in time. It can be, that by the time a lump on the breast is diagnosed as cancerous, two-thirds of its life has already gone by, for it takes 100 million cells to form a lump, and the time interval between one cell and that astronomical figure is about ten years. Abnormal hormone changes in the body can increase cancer and I wonder if, when Mary's weight varied so suddenly in her late twenties, we should not have had her thoroughly examined. A wise doctor friend of hers advised this at the time, but neither of us did anything about it.

Most lumps on the breast are not initially serious, but they have to be removed and studied under a microscope before they can be diagnosed as cancerous or non-cancerous. Mary went to a specialist who ordered her to hospital and operated at once. The lumps were non-malignant and there was no mention of cancer. We breathed a deep sigh of relief. Nevertheless, the specialist advised her to come back every three months for a check-up. She kept doing this, and after about a year or so more lumps appeared on the breast and he operated again; they were still non-malignant, but he strongly advised her to keep coming back every three months for further examinations. For about a a year she kept up these visits regularly and then suddenly stopped. She believed her lumps were ordinary cysts and of no consequence; and she was convinced that she had no cancer, and was only wasting his time. *This was the fatal mistake that ended her life so quickly.* I have since learned that a woman who shows herself susceptible to growths on the breast, even though they are harmless, may very easily develop a malignant one, and this is what happened to Mary.

Of course, I know now that this decision was a monstrous error, and it is almost beyond belief that we were both so utterly stupid. I bitterly reproach myself that I did not firmly insist on her keeping up these regular visits, but never in our married life did I put my foot down or give an ultimatum; neither did she. We lived together respecting each other's opinions and decisions. For the ordinary routine of daily living this, of course, is ideal, but now I realise that there are times, particularly in matters of health, when one or other must insist on the right thing being done. I have also learned since that most women who have these breast lumps checked and attended to regularly can be cured; I learned this too late. Again I reproach myself for not having gone to the specialist and found out for myself; but I just heedlessly and carelessly let things drift. The horror of this neglect is a burden I must carry with me all my life; but no regrets can cure her now; no remorse can bring her back. This was one of those great might-have-been moments that come to pass in the life of every human being where a destiny for good or for evil is settled for all time. The fatal mistake was made, and I must accept and acknowledge my share of the responsibility. Not even God can change the past.

Despite all this stupidity on our part, life went on normally, neither of us knowing that she had signed her death warrant, and that I, through my carelessness and casualness, had countersigned it.

The children were at a stage where they did not make so many demands on our time: Kathleen was at the University; young Mary was a boarder at the Ursuline Convent, Blackrock; Gerald was attending Rockwell Catering School and Sean was apprenticed to an Antique dealer in Dublin. Mary had time on her hands and she threw herself more fully into the work of the Disabled Artists Association, which she had started in Ireland a few years earlier. The Disabled Artists Association is a world wide organisation which helps people who lose the use of their hands to earn their living without depending on charity or handouts. It is not a charitable organisation and it does not accept donations. Virtually its entire revenue comes from the sale of Christmas cards, the originals of which were painted either with the mouth or the foot. This organisation is controlled absolutely by disabled people, who decide all matters of policy and all matters relating to the distribution of earnings, and in each country a representative is appointed who is directly responsible for all activities in that country to the central directorate of disabled people in Switzerland. I was appointed the representative for Ireland, but because of my other work in the publishing house, I handed over the effective running of the organisation in Ireland to Mary. She made a great success of the sale of these Christmas cards in Ireland, and she organised the many exhibitions of the artists' original works in various centres throughout the country. Indeed the last public function she attended before she died was an exhibition of Christy Brown's paintings in July 1970 at the Agnew-Somerville Galleries in Dublin.

The whole conception of the Disabled Artists Association was something which appealed very much to Mary's real sense of values. Here was a group of people, afflicted by the most appalling handicaps, who refused to lie down and accept charity, and who devised a system of earning their living from the sale of their work, in open competition with the best artists in the world. This idea of self-help appealed immensely to her; she had developed a very cautious attitude towards the 'do-gooder' who could be found on the committees of various charitable organisations. Her experience of many of these people was that their activities were mere projections of their own egomania, and the kudos they got out of their image as charity-workers was their sought-for reward. They loved not Truth, but the pleasure Truth could bring them. She saw in the attitude 'we the rich must help the poor' the summit of smugness and selfishness. She herself helped everybody whether they were rich or poor, high or low, and she asked nothing in return. To the needy she gave, and gave without stinting, but nobody was told about it; she was on no committee, and her name never appeared on published lists of donations. Only since she died have I begun to get a glimpse of the extent of her kindness and material help to others, for in the three months after her death hardly a day passed that someone did not ring up, or approach me on the street, to tell me of the help she gave them in time of need. Of all this, I knew nothing while she was alive.

Her work with the Disabled Artists Association was to a large extent seasonal; the months of October, November, December were months of great activity in the sale and dispatch of Christmas cards, but the work tended to ease off after January, and to die out altogether in early Spring.

She now began to take active steps to realise a dream of long standing to start a small business of her own. *The Mercier Press* had grown to the point where it employed a large staff, and the old personal atmosphere of the early pioneering days was gone. She remained a director and attended board meetings, but she felt it was inadvisable for both of us to work daily in the same firm where many experts had to be employed, and where the demarcation lines of responsibilities could be hard to define clearly. She preferred something smaller and more personal for herself.

For a long time she had been a reader and collector of old, rare and out-of-print books, and had studied and researched the markets in this field. So she started an Antiquarian bookshop in Bridge Street which, on one hand, would give added fulfilment to her life and, on the other, would be a useful business to hand over to Sean when he completed his training in Dublin. Sean now runs this bookshop successfully, but we little thought then that he would have to take her place so soon.

Slowly and carefully she built it up and, after initial mistakes and growing pains, it began to prosper. Businesses do not thrive on idleness, and I have seen her, time and again, work long into the night preparing catalogues. As each year passed her clientele of book-buyers increased, and at the time of her death, they were numbered in their thousands in almost all parts of the world. One of the big problems in an Antiquarian bookshop is to keep up a regular supply of old and rare books which have to be bought almost entirely from private houses. Unlike so many bookdealers anxious to make a 'fast buck', Mary paid maximum prices for everything she bought in private houses. Word of this soon spread and people trusted her, so that before her death she was buying more private collections of books than anyone else in the country.

Although this bookshop was a great part of her life, secretly the success of *The Mercier Press* was her first love. She was not now actively associated with it, but she could hardly forget that, together with J. C. O'Connor and myself, she founded it. Twenty-one years had passed since then, and one of the real high points of her life was the celebration dinner for the twenty-first anniversary of the founding of the Press. How well I remember that evening. Hundreds of guests gathered in the great hall of the Imperial Hotel. Everybody who was anybody in the literary world was there. Representatives of the book trade from Germany, Holland, France, England and U.S.A. came to celebrate the success of what one of them called, 'the little provincial firm which had done so much to make the name of Irish writing known throughout the world'. Mary was radiantly happy, and in her shy, retiring way, she welcomed the guests as they came and moved around the groups making everybody feel at ease. Her whole being lit up with joy as she listened to speech after speech praising the work of the Press, and if somebody said something particularly nice about me, I could see her smiling eyes glancing, almost furtively, at me from across the tables. Jack O'Connor and Mary and myself together cut the first slice of a magnificent twenty first anniversary cake. It was our great hour of glory.

Later that night, as the two of us sat by our own fireside, we talked about the early days of the infant publishing house; the difficulties, doubts and failures that are part and parcel of every pioneering effort. Time and again, during those twenty-one years, we were on the verge of collapse, not knowing where the next week's wages were to come from, but somehow we surmounted crisis after crisis and survived. We had gambled with destiny and won; and now, after twenty-one years, we had reached, in many ways, the pinnacle of triumph. Our business ventures were successful, our children were progressing satisfactorily; we felt the joy of fulfilling ourselves through our work, and there was no cloud in the sky.

When I look back on that evening, I am reminded of a poignant scene in Noël Coward's well known play *Cavalcade*. Two young people on their honeymoon are leaning against the deck-rails of a liner at sea. Soft music, a beautiful moonlight night emphasise their love for each other and the happiness of the moment. As they move away, arm in arm, they disclose a lifebelt with the name of the ship *Titanic*. The audience know, of course, that the *Titanic* is doomed; but the young people, oblivious to the immediate death awaiting them, are fully enjoying all the happiness that the evening can bring.

Mary and I, like the young couple on the ship, were enjoying to the full the happiness of that evening, not knowing that her *Titanic* was so very, very close. It is a most merciful God that veils the future from us.

Very shortly after this, I had to go to the United States to mount an exhibition of Mercier Press books in New York. Mary, Kathleen, and young Mary came with me, partly to help at the stand and partly as a holiday. Before the exhibition started, we spent a few days in Maryland, and visited Baltimore, the American naval base at Annapolis, and the battlefield of Gettysburg. She particularly wanted to go to Gettysburg and stand on the spot where Lincoln stood when he made his immortal speech ending with the words which she so often quoted:

> *It is rather for us to be here dedicated to the great task remaining before us, that from these honoured dead we take increased devotion of that cause for which they here gave the last full measure of devotion; that we here highly resolve that the dead shall not have died in vain, that this nation, under God, shall have a new birth of freedom; and that government of the people, by the people and for the people shall not perish from the earth.*

There was still another cemetery she wanted to visit. It was Arlington. Despite the crowd, she knelt at the ever-burning flame and prayed for another American president who was shot dead just a half year before.

When the exhibition was over, we were many times the guests of that great Irish-American industrialist, Jack Mulcahy and his wife, at their beautiful home in Connecticut. They put a car and a guide at our disposal, and through this act of generosity we were able to make many trips into the American countryside at the height of Spring when it was at its most beautiful. Mary was in magnificent form. She sparkled with quiet joy and gaiety and really loved the whole American scene. To visit the U.S.A. was one of her life's ambitions and she had worked hard to realise it. One evening, when we were having dinner with Jack Mulcahy, she told him of a certain uneasiness she had about Kathleen's health, and Jack immediately got in touch with a famous specialist and arranged for Kathleen to see him. She went with her mother and had a complete check-up. The day they went it was on the tip of my tongue to suggest to Mary that she herself have a check-up; why did I not say it? I just do not know. Even then it might not have been too late, and I might have saved her life.

For the next year or so Mary lived a normal, ordinary life; nothing happened to give any cause for anxiety or alarm about her health. In spite of the amount of work she was doing, we found more time to be together, to take long walks in the country on the week-ends, to sail in Summer around Cork Harbour, to fish a little on the Blackwater, and in the evenings to go to the theatre. In the summer of 1966, she herself and young Mary joined a tour for a short holiday in Italy. That Autumn saw her in magnificent form, looking younger than ever with her Mediterranean tan. The winter months came and on November 16th we celebrated Kathleen's twenty-first birthday.

Mary busied herself with the work of the Disabled Artists Association, which was now in full swing. Christmas came, and, during the holidays, when she should have been relaxed, I sensed a slight change in the barometer of her demeanour, but I asked no questions. I knew that whatever it was, she would tell me in her own good time.

On New Year's Day we went for a walk through the woods at Currabinny. It was a quiet road unfrequented by cars, so that we were able to let the poodles loose to frolic and gambol to their hearts content. After walking some time in silence in the sharp frosty air, she quietly broke the news:

'I have found more lumps on my breast,' she said. 'I have seen the specialist and he is going to operate again.'

I cannot say that I was unduly alarmed, as already she had had two operations on the breast and the lumps proved harmless. Surely this was merely a recurrence and nothing serious to worry about? When I said this to her she seemed unsure and hesitant.

'He found another lump under my arm,' she said, 'and I sensed he was not happy about it; although he did not say so, it might be cancerous.'

Rather flippantly I dismissed the whole idea as ridiculous. 'You are far too healthy looking to have cancer,' I said. Nevertheless, for days and weeks afterwards, I could not help thinking she might be right. If she were, what then? How far gone was it? Could it be stopped? And here I indulged in an illusion that I was stupidly to repeat over and over again: I knew many women who were operated on for cancer, and who were alive and healthy fifteen or sixteen years afterwards. Had I examined that notion, with even a fraction of the care I would examine a business proposition, I would have found out, as I found out after her death, that these women whom I knew were either taken in time or indeed had no cancer at all. It is not only ostriches who hide their heads in the sand.

The day I brought her to the nursing home she seemed nervous and unsure. We drove in silence through the city streets and, when she had registered, I brought her suit-cases to her room, and as she prepared to go to bed I prepared to leave. 'Come to see me as often as you can,' were her parting words to me.

Early the following morning she was operated on, and I visited her in the afternoon, which was the soonest they would allow me to see her. She was still very drowsy so I stayed only a few moments. As I was about to leave, she smiled, held out her hand weakly to me, and said: 'Come back to-morrow.'

When I got to my office, a message to ring the surgeon awaited me; this was unusual. I got through to his secretary and she told me he would like to see me, and when I asked for an appointment, she said to come along at any time. This I thought very strange. He is a most eminent surgeon, and it normally takes three or four weeks to get an appointment, but here was his secretary more or less saying 'drop in any time and he will see you': 'You don't need an appointment,' she said.

'What about now?' I asked.

'That will be fine,' she answered.

There and then I went to his consulting rooms, which were only a few minutes away from my office. I was not shown to the waiting room, which I could see was crowded, but instead I was given a seat in the hallway. When he was free, I was shown into his surgery. We shook hands and he sat me down in an armchair.

'The news is not too good,' he said, 'I have operated on the breast and under the arm and I am afraid it looks as if the growths are malignant. As yet it is hard to say how far it has gone, but to be on the safe side, I propose to operate again in a few days and remove her ovaries.' He spoke kindly and gently, almost in a fatherly way.

I was stunned. Although I was somewhat anxious over the past few weeks, I was entirely unprepared for this. The significance of taking out the ovaries I did not understand, but it sounded frightening and I immediately thought the worst.

'Does this mean that she is going to die?' I asked bluntly.

'Not necessarily,' he answered. 'But if any vital organ were to become affected, then it would be dangerous.'

'How long is she going to live?' I asked, pressing the point home.

'It is difficult to say,' he answered. 'But I propose to put her on radiation treatment after the operation, and we will see how that works.'

I had to be satisfied with this much information, and as I was leaving he shook my hand warmly and said: 'We will look after her well.'

I came out into the street to a different world from that which I left behind me going in. The material world and activity was the same, but I saw it differently, or indeed it would be nearer the truth to say that I did not see it at all. People, cars, traffic, went by as if I were only dreaming about them. I made my way back to the office and sat down. The telephone was ringing but I did not answer. Reality had dawned on me. Mary had cancer. It was spreading. She was going to die—of that I was now certain. If there were no danger of death the surgeon would have said so clearly. I imagined he would have said: 'For heaven's sake have sense, man. There is no question of death.' But he did not. He was cautious and indefinite. In effect what he said was that everything possible would be done for her but there was no certainty. The big question now was: when would she die?

In our bookshop, which was just under my office, we have a large section of medical textbooks, so I went down and picked out a standard work on cancer. After almost an hour's study, I learned that cancer is a disorder which in some of the cells of the body just go berserk; they spread through various parts, forming what are known as secondary deposits. These, if they effect a vital organ, are fatal. The present method of treating cancer is by surgery and radiation. Radiation damages the cancerous cell and prevents it from spreading; but the trouble here is that the cells may have spread so widely that radiation can only treat a fraction. Worst of all, I read that *most women with cancer of the breast were found to have an average duration of life of* $4\frac{3}{12}$ *years, even if operated on and treated by radiation.*

A sickening emptiness came over me as I read all this, getting worse as I progressed from sentence to sentence. People who had appointments with me called but I was simply unable to see anyone. I could only think 'Mary is going to die', 'Mary is going to die'. I left the office without explanation and drove out into the country. Everything was bare and cold. Incapable of thinking or feeling clearly, I walked aimlessly on the country roads for more than an hour, and when tiredness had steadied me up a bit, I slowly drove home. Young Mary had come home from the convent school for the day, and Kathleen was back from the University. They had both been to see their mother for a few minutes. I told them what the surgeon had said, and what I had read in the cancer book, as I do not believe in the phoney kindness of keeping a necessary and vital truth from those most intimately concerned. This is cowardice, not kindness; we were one family closely united in love; why should we not be united in sorrow too? They took everything calmly, and after a long silence Kathleen said: 'I really hope she does not have too much pain.' There were no tears—just that brave silence of acceptance.

Time had now begun to move. It was then January 1967. The longest Mary could live was April 1971. Just two months short of that date she died.

In the days and weeks that followed, I said nothing to Mary herself about my talk with the specialist. I would wait until she was home for a few weeks before breaking the news. How I was going to do so I did not clearly see, but I felt that in some way a suitable intimate opportunity would come. She got over the second operation and some time afterwards she was discharged. At home we had a blazing log fire awaiting her, and she was thrilled to be back. The poodles jumped all over her with joy, trying to lick her face and hands, and her favourite, Hoppy, refused to leave her arms. She did not go to bed immediately, but sat by the fire listening to us telling everything, big and small, important and unimportant, that happened while she was gone. She made a quick inspection of the house, praising us for some improvements, and good-humouredly chiding us for some neglect. Altogether it was a happy evening, and no outsider looking on would ever think that three of us knew she was going to die; at least we thought only three of us knew. Very soon I was to learn that the fourth, herself, knew too.

Later that night, when she had gone to bed, I sat by the bedside talking to her.

'You were with the surgeon,' she said. This took me unawares.

'I was,' I answered, after some hesitation.

'I am going to die.' She spoke these words calmly.

'He was not by any means as definite as that,' I said. There was a long pause.

'Don't try to fool me, Sean, I have my own ways of finding things out. I have cancer. It is spreading. With luck I have four to five years to live.'

I knew it was pointless asking her where she got her information; she would not tell. Again it was too accurate to contradict. Before I had time to say anything, she continued:

'There is something else. My ovaries have been removed, and this means that my menopause has been forced on me many years before its time. As you know, women going through the menopause are difficult, depressive, irritating, and troublesome. I will do my best to avoid being like that, but should I fail, I want to ask your forgiveness in advance. Do not be hurt at what I do or say. I love the children, but I love you more than anything in the world. Always remember that.'

She turned her head away to hide the tears in her eyes, and I hurriedly left the room to hide the tears in mine.

Life had now thrown out its most terrible challenge and she had accepted with the supreme courage of an immortal. Mary loved life and everything about it, and now she was condemned to death—one of the most painful deaths possible. She would have to live, day in day out, with this shadow over her. She had not even the consolation of her womanhood; this was taken from her too, threatening the possibility of mental unbalance, depressions, and strange psychic illnesses. Could there be a more gloomy prospect?

The little girl from Clare, Mary Kissane, whom I fell in love with so long ago, who came to Cork with two battered suit-cases and a ten-pound note, now faced a life that could shatter the greatest of humans, and smash the spirit of even the strongest souls. How would she face it?

Like a Greek goddess rising from the seas, she soared high above it. She had the courage to face this new and terrible life and make something great of it, in a way that inspired those who knew her with hope, joy, confidence in the mercy of God and the greatness of the human spirit. What should have been the four worst years of her life became the four greatest and most glorious. No matter how painful and depressing a future loomed ahead, she transcended it with sweetness, patience, gentleness, and bravery.

Pain is essentially loneliness. It cannot be shared with others. We must carry our cross alone. No matter how much we loved her, how close we were to her, how deeply committed we were, she had to face every minute, every hour, every day of those agonising years, by herself alone, culminating in the supreme loneliness of the hour of death.

'Some are born great; others have greatness thrust upon them.' The hidden greatness in her life now came to the surface and this terrible blow failed to destroy the core of her being. The great reality that was Mary remained untouched. Through the life she lived the black emptiness of death was overcome and her final moment of triumph was just around the corner. Truth, she often said, always wins the last battle, and as far as is possible in the human condition, she was completely at one with Truth. She could now rejoice with the poet:

Halts by me that footfall:
Is my gloom after all,
Shade of His hand, outstretched caressingly . . . ?

Chapter Four

I hear the drops of my life falling one by one into the devouring abyss of eternity. I feel my days flying before the pursuit of death. All that remains of weeks, months, or years, in which I may drink in the light of the sun, seems no more than a single summer night which will soon be at an end.

Amiel

The Requiem Mass was to be celebrated at 11 a.m. in Ballinlough Church on February 16th, the day of her burial. All that morning there was an avalanche of telegrams, telephone calls and letters. The notice in the papers which said 'House Private' was largely ignored. The first telegram to arrive was from An Taoiseach, Mr. Jack Lynch, and this was quickly followed by other telegrams, letters, and calls from all parts of the country, and from an amazingly wide number of walks of life.

. . . she was one of the loveliest women I ever met . . .

. . . her spirit sounded as good as ever during the phone conversation I had with her a few weeks ago . . .

. . . she radiated goodness without being goody-good . . .

. . . we only met Mary once but that was enough to reveal her gentle goodness . . .

. . . what a lovely person she was . . . so kind, so sincere . . .

. . . and what courage she had. I never suspected how really ill she was . . .

. . . it seems impossible to believe that anyone so young looking and attractive could be gone. . . .

. . . although we met Mary only once we will always remember her kindness and her dignity . . .

. . . she had such a sweet and gentle disposition, offending none, and while by nature retiring, still possessed a mind very much her own . . .

. . . she was so young and lovely . . .

. . . she was such a gentle, kind and dignified woman. It is hard to believe she is no longer with us and still harder to understand why she had to leave this world so soon . . .

. . . you built up many things together, not the least the now famous Mercier Press, but there must have been many ups and downs, and perhaps stumbles too, before the peak was reached. To have achieved so much together makes it all the harder now when you must go it alone . . .

. . . she was your all, and life will be so empty without her unfailing help. But keep on being in touch with her, talk to her every day and confide in her all your worries and needs . . . she is nearer than ever to you now . . .

There were hundreds of them, all saying much the same thing; all recalling her goodness, her gentleness, her dignity, her courage. It was only as I re-read through them that it became clear to me what an impact she made on everyone who met her. I had taken her great virtues for granted. Strangers had seen them with greater clarity, and now I was about to pay the price of my blindness.

My brother James, who is a priest in the diocese of Cashel, said the requiem mass. I knelt with the four children, in the front row, in sight of her coffin; it was quite beyond me to realise that she lay lifeless there. I had gone to funerals many times with her; together we had prayed at other requiem masses for other people; it was always others. Now it was us. Now it was Mary. Death was no longer an outside event; it had struck home.

Somewhere in the distance I heard James reading the beautiful prayer before communion:

> *Remember Mary. In Baptism she died with Christ, may she also share his resurrection, when Christ will raise our mortal bodies and make them like his own in glory. . . . When every tear will be wiped away.*

I know that during the Mass I should have been more prayerful; I should have felt that God had taken over, taken Mary to him and opened up for me a new, but veiled, life without her physical presence. Intellectually I accepted the theology of Hope, that she was now in a condition which should be the envy of every human being, that she was totally penetrated through and through with a happiness and fulfilment unknown on this earth, that what to our puny minds seemed to be the end was the real beginning, but right then the human element in me was on top. My mind and soul were numb. Somehow God, eternity, the world around me did not exist; I had become, unknown to myself, depersonalised. There were moments when I lapsed into day-dreaming and thought it was not Mary's funeral, it was someone else's; at times I expected her to take my arm and say, 'Sean, come, let's go to the car.' But then I would awake to the reality, the coffin, the flowers, the children and friends in mourning black.

There is so little I can now remember of the happenings of that morning, of the good friends who came and prayed and shook our hands. Mechanically I must have thanked them and quickly made my way to the security of the car.

I can only recall the torturing pain within me; I did not realise then that it was but a mild foretaste of what was to come.

*

Dearest Mary: Today, one of the wildest and wettest days of the year, brought back memories of the last sad weeks of your life. Exactly a year ago today you had just two weeks to live. In daylight and in darkness you lay on your bed of pain, sometimes gently sleeping, sometimes just thinking with a far-away look in your eyes. But all the time, day and night, your favourite dog, Hoppy, was curled up beside you, his tiny sensitive head resting gently on your weak, helpless arm. He was so loyal to you and loved you so much. Just a few hours ago, in the blinding rain, I had to dig his grave. I dug it beneath the, window of your bedroom under the laurels, where in summer he used to lie in shelter from the scorching sun. After your death he went to pieces. At every opportunity he jumped on to your bed searching for you, and when he could not find you he began to whine and moan and cry. He wandered aimlessly around the house, sniffing and smelling, and sometimes just standing on all fours staring into space almost like a human. Other times, I found him asleep beside your bed, his head resting on your slippers. It was with great difficulty we got him to eat his food. He had two heart attacks and we barely saved his life. Then he slowly went completely blind, and it was pathetic to see him bumping into everything as he hobbled along. As I was digging his grave he heard the noise of the spade, and moving towards it hesitantly, he fell head first into the open earth.

He slept with me every night in the bed, his head resting on my arm as it rested on yours during your last days. As far as I could I brought him everywhere I went, to the office, to Dublin, to Longfield. But as time went on he got worse and developed, like yourself, cancer, and to ease his sufferings we had to put him down. Leonore called in her car to bring him to the veterinary surgeon. I carried him in my arms around to Mary and Kathleen to say good-bye. At the door I hugged him, long and lovingly, and handed him over to be brought to his death. Leonore was away an hour; what a terrible hour it was. I remembered again and again the great joy and happiness he gave you throughout his short life, so that sometimes you would say he was nearer to you than a human. His frail little body came back in a small green sack which I laid gently on the dark earth, and covered it as quickly as possible to ease the pain in my own heart. I took off his collar and put it in the little glass case where all my souvenirs of you are kept; your sun-glasses, your rosary, your gloves, your necklaces, your small jewelry, your birth certificate, our marriage certificate, and a hundred other little things I have gathered together in memory of you. One more link in our lives is now broken. One more living joy shared with you is gone. Is it too much to hope that he is with you, or is this another illusion that adds one more pain, one more hurt, on the long hard road of daily life?

★

I suppose the supreme tribute one could pay to the goodness of Mary's life was how little she changed in those last four years; there was so little that needed to be changed. I am reminded here of a story told to me in childhood concerning Ignatius of Loyola who was asked, while playing croquet, what he would do if he knew for certain that he was to die almost immediately. Ignatius replied that he would continue playing croquet. The point of the story was that if our lives are right, we do not have to change when death approaches. Mary, like Ignatius, would continue to live the life she had always lived, with one big difference. When Ignatius made his answer he knew perfectly well that death was not imminent. When Mary made her own answer to life she knew perfectly well that it was.

'I know it, I accept it, but I find it hard to grasp, hard to see as a reality,' she said.

But changes had to be made; not in fundamentals, but in routine. After the operation she was able to move her left arm, but it had lost most of its power. So that she could continue driving we changed cars and got one with automatic gears and automatic window openers, which, I am quite sure, made many of our friends think, at the time, that this was merely status seeking, when in fact it was the best I could offer to ease Mary's pain and make the last years of her life as pleasant as possible. There were many material comforts which I organised for her, and this seemed to give a lot of people the impression that we were wealthy. In fact we were not. When a family works hard, does not habitually drink, smoke or gamble, it is astonishing how much money can be available for other things. I normally came home at midday for lunch which Mary cooked, but now we began to have our midday meal in restaurants, in the County Club, or sometimes take just a snack in the bookshop. I engaged a daily woman to look after the house, and a handy-man to do the garden, lawn, and flowers once a week; Mary was no longer able for any real physical work.

She started the radiation treatment and was able to drive herself daily to the clinic, but this treatment was so severe that she could only take it for a week at a time, and then only at intervals of a month or sometimes two. It had the effect of further depressing her, and she found it soothing to go to bed and rest after it. Occasionally when I came home unexpectedly, I found her crying.

'I am depressed,' she'd say. 'I don't know why. I just am. But it will pass. Forgive me.' There was no irritability or unpleasantness. She seemed to have put all that behind her. Her serenity was in full bloom.

One afternoon I came home and found her sleeping with her head on its side, resting on the pillow. She was whispering something in her sleep. I bent down close to her and heard the pathetic words: 'I do not want to die . . . I do not want to die . . .'

As weeks passed into months and months into years, we became slowly more used to the cloud hanging over us. We began to go a lot to places together, and whenever it was possible she now came with me on business trips. During those long hours driving together we spoke with more freedom to each other than ever before. She talked a great deal about herself, her life, her worries, that in the kindness of her heart she had never troubled me with. She began to unfold slowly her own beautiful mind and soul in a light that I had not seen before. She talked about life's deepest problems, happiness, death, resurrection, love, the whole meaning and purpose of living, in a way that quite astonished me. I always knew she had great depth, but now I was finding a richness of beauty and goodness, the existence of which I had only suspected. Why is it that so many of us have to wait until tragedy strikes to get really close to each other? Why is it that we cannot be that way all our lives? What strange quirk of nature always twists our love until it is too late? I think it was the great Albert Schweitzer who remarked: 'What a terrible reflection on our lives that we say things at a grave which would have meant so much more in life.'

She was, too, so sane and calm, and her approach to the

problems and difficulties of life became less and less urgent. Some people, if they know they are going to die, try to squeeze the last particle of pleasure out of life, but Mary took a calmer and more relaxed view, as if she were moving forward to a life of infinite beauty, which she knew or had a foretaste of, and saw in the pleasures of this life something barren and futile.

'I am not particularly anxious to experience every last experience of this life,' she said. 'I now know most of them are hollow and empty. I only want to be with you and as close to you as possible.'

Sometimes she quoted Oscar Wilde's saying, 'All my life I have sought pleasure and pleasure is so sad'. 'One should not seek pleasure in life,' she said reflectively. 'One should only seek joy. The difference is immense.'

In 1968 we took a holiday together in the Wye valley in Wales, and from our base at Ross-on-Wye we motored through the beautiful Welsh countryside, through mountains, valleys, rushing streams, and waterfalls. We made occasional sorties to Richard Booth's Antiquarian bookshop in Hay-on-Wye, each time coming away with armfuls of books. She was carefree and contented, no pain, no suffering, and it was hard to believe that she was walking in the shadow of death.

The following year, we went for a week to London with young Mary, and here we spent most of our time just wandering through Antique shops and Antiquarian bookshops, and at night seeing the various stage shows which we were unlikely to see in Ireland. I think the highlight of this visit was a day we spent in Oxford. She had never been there and she looked forward to it with unconcealed delight. One of our friends, a Mercier author, Father Yarnold, Master of Campion Hall, was our guide, and he escorted us through the old part of the city, the various colleges, All Souls, Balliol, Christ Church, Oriel, Queen's College, giving us a brief history of each one, and now and then illuminating what he had to say with a bright flash of humour. We felt we were part of a thousand years of learning and culture. Before we left for London, he invited us to tea in the historic Campion Hall, and showed us through the building, with all its relics of the past.

In the train back to London, Mary kept gazing out of the window, strangely silent and reflective, and when I asked her what was on her mind, she answered, still looking away in the distance:

'All who made possible the beautiful buildings of Oxford are gone and forgotten. The hundreds of young people we saw walking there to-day have not even a thought for them. How empty is life!' And then she quoted from Omar Khayyám:

The worldly hope men set their hearts upon
Turns ashes—or it prospers; and anon
Like snow upon the desert's dusty face
Lighting a little hour or two—is gone

I did not answer, but in my mind I recalled another verse of Omar Khayyám, though I did not quote it aloud:

Come, fill the cup, and in the fire of Spring
The winter garment of repentance fling;
The bird of Time has but a little way
To fly—and lo! the bird is on the wing.

The bird had started its short flight. Time was running out.

It was in the Spring of 1970 that she began to experience the first real cancer pains. She continued her radiation treatment, and although this was severe, it helped to relieve the pains; but she could only take a limited amount. The pains came and went; they would last a few days, and then go away, and then return again.

Early that summer we had our last holiday together, and I imagine we both vaguely knew it was to be our last, but we blinded ourselves with false hopes. Maybe it was not as bad as we thought? Maybe the radiation was killing the cancerous cells and this was the cause of the pain? Maybe the researchers would find some magic serum that would effect an immediate cure . . . Maybe . . . Maybe . . .

The reality was that she had seven months to live.

Kathleen and young Mary came with us. We crossed to Swansea on the car-ferry, drove to Hay-on-Wye, where we stayed the night and following day with Elizabeth and Richard Booth in their beautiful country home outside the village. We then motored to Holyhead, where young Mary and I joined some friends on a yacht, the *Cliperau,* for a three-day cruise to the Isle of Man. (As I was revising this chapter, the news came that the *Cliperau* was lost on the way back from a cruise to Gibraltar, with all hands, including our dear friend Bill Tack.) Mary and Kathleen stayed in Holyhead and made day excursions to the seaside resorts of North Wales and at the end of a week we returned to Cork through Liverpool and Dublin. Physically she was now a changed woman. The pains were more frequent and severe, and she could no longer drive the car or lift anything with her left hand.

I made a further change in the routine of my life. At home I converted my study into a kind of office and I did most of my work there. I only went to the Press for two or three hours a day, to meet people or to discuss problems with various members of the staff, while the rest of the time I worked at home, where I was available to her at any moment. If the afternoons were particularly fine, and she was not in too much pain, we motored to Crosshaven and we went aboard our sailing boat, *Inis Ealga,* which was at anchor in the harbour. (After her death we changed the name of the boat to *Dualla.*) I worked inside the cabin on the little chart table, while she lay outside in the sun, and if the pain got particularly bad I would go out on deck, sit and talk to her or read poetry aloud, or maybe brew a cup of tea on the primus. During those beautiful summer afternoons, listening to the sad lapping of the sea against the boat, and the lonely sound of the wind in the rigging, I began to understand a little about sickness and pain. For the first time in my life, I had really come face to face with it. All during the last year of her life, I had to perform tasks which had always seemed to me unpleasant and distasteful. The little bowl, which she constantly carried around with her in case she vomited, had to be emptied repeatedly and cleaned. She had to be brought to the toilet. The bed-chair near her bed had, too, to be emptied and cleaned. Instead of revolting me, these tasks brought me a great sense of fulfilment. During my life I have been given many honours and privileges, but the greatest of all was the privilege of being able to share those sad intimate moments with her. I do not say these things with conceit; I merely state them as simple facts. Sickness is a great teacher for one who comes to grips with it. It penetrates life. It reminds us of life's end and it is a warning not to forget life's real values. It teaches us to feel for the pain in others and to share that pain throughout our lives; not only physical pain, but the pain of sorrow, of loneliness, of despair. When one suffers, we all suffer in some strange way.

If the week-ends were fine, we slipped anchor and sailed around Cork harbour, with Doreen, Claire, and Edmund Hayes who came with us to help. Mary was not always in constant pain, and she would sometimes have very good days completely free from all discomfort, but other times on these week-ends the pain would strike suddenly and we would have to prop her up with pillows until we came ashore.

She was hoping to come with us on our annual cruise down the south-west coast of Cork, but when the day of departure came, she was completely unable for the trip. We sailed the boat to Baltimore and there anchored for the rest of the summer. Most week-ends we motored down from Cork, stayed aboard, and cruised around the various harbours in that delightful corner of Ireland: Cape Clear, Schull, Crookhaven and Carbery's hundred isles. She enjoyed sleeping aboard, waking to the sound of lapping water, having breakfast on deck in the glorious sunshine, and making those short trips in such magnificent surroundings.

But the pains came intermittently, all the time, slowly increasing in intensity.

There were times when she was unable to make the car journey to Baltimore; so, a month earlier than usual, we sailed the boat back to Cork, and as we had favourable winds we arrived a day earlier than expected, When I got home I found she had gone to Dublin for the day by train. This was typical of the pain at the time; it would vanish completely for a few days, enabling her to move about fairly normally, and then return.

This was August 16th. She spent most of the day with Maire O'Donnell, the Abbey actress, who was one of the few women in the world to whom she gave her confidence. She was never to see Dublin again.

There are some people who radiate happiness and joy wherever they go and in whatever painful situation they find themselves. They have the great gift of being able to lift suffering humans out of their desolation and bring the light of hope back to their eyes. Maire O'Donnell was one of these gifted people. During the last year of Mary's painful illness, Maire came regularly to Cork and stayed with us for long periods.

For hours on end she sat by Mary's bedside and, in my study which was just underneath, I could hear the brilliant conversation, witty repartee, interspersed with happy laughter as they exchanged their thoughts. In Maire's magic presence, the sparkle of life came back to Mary and I know that were it not for her unselfish kindness, Mary could have died long before she did.

Kathleen was engaged for about a year to a young Cork dentist, Paudie Barrett, and they were married at the Honan Chapel, U.C.C., on August 29th. Mary's pain was particularly severe on that beautiful and happy day, but the painkillers prescribed by the doctors made it bearable. After the wedding festivities were over and the young couple had gone on their honeymoon, we went to Kinsale with Mary and Mick Heffernan for a quiet meal, although she would have liked to join the main wedding party who were putting a gay and hilarious end to the day in Blarney, but she was exhausted and the effect of the drugs was beginning to wear off.

October came with its cold sharp night air, and towards the end of the month she became very ill. Her *via dolorosa* was about to begin in earnest, as she entered the dark, raw world of depression, uncertainty and gloom—the prelude to death. The pains spread throughout her body and increased in intensity, and more and stronger drugs were needed; now a new cause for concern appeared. She was unable to keep her food down and vomited almost every meal.

'The pains rack my body,' she said, 'and I am getting no nutrition to resist. I cannot stay alive much longer.'

As far as was humanly possible, I arranged for members of the staff to see and deal with authors, publishers, and other callers whom I would normally have to meet, so that I could spend more and more time with Mary. Each day I worked at home in the study, and every hour or so I went to her room to see how she was, or talk, or maybe read a little to her. I now asked myself regularly 'Is she dying?' and my intellect would answer 'Yes'. And my heart would say 'No, she will pull out of it.' Emotionally, I suppose, I was unable to bear the thought of her death and I just kept deluding myself in the face of every reality. But I did realise that the most important single thing I could now do for her was to show her all my love, compassion, understanding, and tenderness, which could help to relieve the spiritual and intellectual desolation which engulfed her. This I tried to give wholeheartedly and without reserve, although I began to realise that it had all come too late, that I should have given it to her throughout all her life. I now fully understood St. Augustine's despairing cry: 'Too late have I loved you, O beauty of beauties. Too late have I loved you.'

She now had no illusions about herself and she knew that death was very near. I am still awed by her attitude towards death. The thought of death frightens even the bravest, but for Mary it seemed to hold no terrors; she saw it as a transition point, at which one existence ended, and a new form of the same existence began. Her concern during those last months was not for herself, but for others: that I might be able to attend to my business affairs; that young Mary might be able to study for her final University examination; that she herself would not be a burden or annoyance to anyone. By these small actions, she emphasised the importance of life to those who had to live after her. She was completely unselfish to the last.

By mid-November I was getting really alarmed. The pain was now severe and constant in almost all parts of her body, and I went to see the specialist who ordered her to hospital at once. She wanted to be alone in the hospital, so we had to wait almost a week before a private room became available. The day I brought her in she was able to walk upstairs to her room.

I helped her to her bed, and when she settled herself in, I got ready to leave. As I was saying good-bye she held on to my hand and said: 'Sean, come to see me often, I do not think I will ever leave here alive.' I could not speak. I bent down, kissed her and held her close to me, and then quickly left the room.

She spent ten days in hospital, during which various treatments were tried and various tests taken. The pain eased a lot and the vomiting became less and less frequent, and I thought she was on the way to recovery, but she was the greater realist. 'It is only the drugs,' she said, 'I am not cured.'

I saw the specialist again and he held out no great hope. On the question of how long she would live he did not like to express an opinion. One has to realise that doctors are in no way alarmists; they put things as gently and as hopefully as possible, but when they are uncertain and hesitant, it is time to look out. This man had done everything possible for Mary but now there was nothing more he could do.

When I brought her home from the hospital, she managed to walk slowly, with the aid of a stick, into the house. I had a bright, cheery fire lighting for her, and, as she sat in the armchair, her dog Hoppy kept jumping up and down on her lap letting out little cries of delight and trying to lick her hands and face. She was thrilled to be home again.

'It's wonderful to be back,' she said. 'I never believed I would see this room again.' And in a more jocose mood: 'Well, Hoppy, are you glad to see me back? Say "Welcome home,"' and Hoppy barked and barked until she took him and snuggled him in her arms.

I brought her to the clinic for radiation treatment on the prescribed days. Here a new world opened up to me as I watched the patients coming and going one by one, in cars, taxis, and ambulance, hobbling in pain into the hall, or being wheeled in on a wheel-chair by kind and gentle nurses. How many of them are now alive? During the Christmas period four of those who attended with Mary died. It is no wonder that the doctor and staff of the clinic are kindness itself. Dealing hourly and daily with poor human beings, desperately trying to cling on to life, must give them a rare understanding and insight into human pain; their eyes see so much hope, and so much heartbreak.

When she left the clinic, if she were in form and if the days were fine, we went for a short drive before going home. We usually drove to the seaside at Fountainstown and sat listening to the sound of the waves breaking on the shore. Sometimes, sitting there, I recalled the past, when, on that very same strand, she played and swam with the children, and now she was back again, in the last days of her life, crippled and unable to move. One day as we sat there she said to me:

'Sean, I'll never walk again. Even if I live I will be absolutely useless to you.'

The painful despairing voice in which she spoke those words touched me deeply.

'I married you because I loved you, Mary,' I answered with emotion, 'not because of the use you could be to me. And at this moment I love you more than ever before and more than anything or anyone in the world.' She painfully put her frail, wasted hand into mine and burst into tears.

On December 11th she suffered a great shock when the news came that Paddy Hughes, manager of our Dublin office, had died suddenly. Only a few days before she had spoken to him on the phone; Paddy and herself were old friends and his death upset her deeply. She insisted that I go to Dublin for the two days of the funeral, as young Mary could look after her. Before he died, Paddy recorded for Radio Eireann a series of short spiritual talks under the general heading *Thought for To-day,* and shortly after his death they were broadcast each morning, for a week, and Mary listened to every one of them, to his familiar voice, almost with a sense of foreboding.

On Christmas Day 1970 she was able to come down to dinner. Kathleen's husband Paudie, was reading a post-graduate course in dentistry at Dundee University in Scotland, and they had gone there immediately after their wedding, but both of them managed to come home for Christmas. We all sat by the fire most of the afternoon, talking and chatting, yet there was an air of slight unreality about the whole day. We knew, including herself, that it would be her last Christmas on this earth, and this unspoken and suppressed knowledge made free conversation difficult, so we spent a lot of the time looking at the Christmas television programmes. At tea-time she went to bed; the pain had returned.

One of my saddest memories is that of New Year's Eve, the last night of 1970. The two of us were alone in the house, and as midnight approached we were sitting by the fire, she in her dressing-gown, listening to a concert. At midnight I got up and opened the hall door. Suddenly all hell was let loose. Bells, factory horns, ships' sirens, car hooters, everything that could make noise was saying farewell to the old year and welcoming in the new; revellers in the street were merrily singing *Should Auld Acquaintance Be Forgot.* Suddenly I realised that she was listening too, as she had listened to it every year for twenty-six years, and I realised that she would never hear it again. I lingered on a little outside the door so that she would not notice anything, but as I crossed the threshold a cold shiver went down my spine, and a lonesome kind of fear chilled me to the bone. Never again would we ring out the old year and ring in the new together. She was sitting forward with her head resting in her hands, her hair hanging loosely over her arms. The room was silent. All the noise had stopped. After what seemed an age, she slowly raised her head, looked strangely at me for a moment and then said:

'Sean, dear, could you help me up to bed?'

A few days later she was feeling well enough to get up and dress herself, come to town, and together we walked slowly around and did a little shopping. In a seed shop she bought some snowdrops and crocus bulbs, and when we got home she planted them on the lawn. This was a brave gesture of hope. Months later, when Spring was bursting over the earth, I picked those delicate snowdrops and put them on her grave.

Every morning I got up early and brought her breakfast, which consisted of a sliced sour apple, a little bacon, and a cup of tea. During the day she ate mostly fruit and drank pure fruit juices. However, when she had a good day, she would dress herself and I would drive her to a restaurant where she could eat a full meal; most of the time she was unable to keep it down. Twice a day I partially carried her, partially walked her to the toilet. Teresa MacSweeney, one of our kind neighbours, came up and washed her daily, and she then either stayed in bed or sat by the fire downstairs, depending on how she felt. I usually worked then until seven, when young Mary returned from the University and prepared supper; afterwards I sat with her, either talking or reading, until long after midnight. Then, when the drugs began to take effect and she got a little sleep, I would tumble exhausted into my bed.

But sometimes the drugs would not work, or the pain would be too severe. Then I would prop her up in the bed, surrounded by pillows, and change her every now and then as the pains moved around her body; after a while she might tell me to go to bed, that there was no more I could do, and that she would only have to bear the pain. What were her thoughts throughout those lonely nights of agony when she could not sleep? Did she feel her life fleeing away before the onrush of death?

Did she think about another possible world? Did she see only mystery and uncertainty on all sides, and her faith the only light in this terrible darkness? Or did she think of all the happiness she brought to others, all the sorrowful she helped and comforted, all the unselfish devotion and love she spread around her during her life? Whatever her thoughts were she never expressed them, but pondered everything in the silence of her own soul.

Then there came odd days when she was on top of the world, no pain, no vomiting, no depression. I recall one of those days, just three weeks before she died. When I brought her breakfast she told me how wonderful she felt, and I said impulsively: 'Let's go down to Tipperary shooting. We'll bring Deelish along and you'll see him working'. She was overjoyed. I helped her get up and dress. She put on her best clothes and fur coat. We drove along the road to Cashel where we had lunch. (The next time I would drive along this road, a few weeks later, would be behind her coffin.) I thought of going to Dualla but I changed my mind, and went instead to Ballyboe, at the foot of Slievenamon, where we had a week-end cottage. Deelish was our Irish red setter and she loved to see him work, search, and 'set' the pheasant and snipe. It was a beautiful day. The sky was clear and the sun was shining. There was a light frosty nip in the air. The grass under our feet was soft and crisp. A fresh north-easterly breeze blew down from the mountain and across the green fields. But after about half an hour she felt she had had enough. On our way back to the car we met Jack Tobin, a local farmer, who invited us to his house where Mary was delighted to get a large glass of her favourite drink, fresh buttermilk. We stayed only a short while with Jack and his family and then drove home.

Back in Cork she was much weaker and the pains returned. 'It was too much for me,' she said.

During the weeks following, she got weaker and weaker,

lapsed back into pain and vomiting, and I now stayed in the room with her almost continually. When she slept I dozed on the chair. When she was awake, and in pain, I read to her, mostly poetry. Again and again she asked me to read one particular poem, Alan Seeger's *Rendezvous,* and it seemed to have a peculiar poignant meaning for her:

I have a rendezvous with Death . . .
When Spring comes back with rustling shade
And apple blossoms fill the air,
I have a rendezvous with Death
When Spring brings back blue days and fair
It may be he shall take my hand,
And lead me into his dark land
And close my eyes and quench my breath
It may be I shall pass him still.
I have a rendezvous with Death . . .
When Spring comes 'round again this year
And the first meadow flowers appear . . .
I have a rendezvous with Death . . .
When Spring trips north again this year
And I to my pledged world am true
I shall not fail that rendezvous.

Spring was tripping north again, blue days and fair were coming, apple blossoms would soon fill the air, and the first meadow flowers appear. Her rendezvous was getting closer and closer, day by day.

One day she made a peculiar request. She asked me to buy her a present of Brindsley MacNamara's *Valley of the Squinting Windows.* I got it for her and she began to read it slowly, very slowly; she could only read a page or two and would then have to rest. I wondered why she wanted this particular book, as I had a hazy recollection that she read it before, and when she did not offer to tell me, I did not ask. It was only after her death I got a clue. In her little private safe, where she kept all her letters, I found a letter which I had written to her, just after our engagement in September 1944. It contained the following sentence:

> I am sending you under separate cover a book called *The Valley of the Squinting Windows.* Read it. I know you will enjoy it.

It was the first gift I ever gave her. Did she want the same book to be my last gift?

Tuesday, the 9th February 1971 is a day of poignant memory. I brought her breakfast as usual and found her in the top of her form; all her pains had vanished. She ate heartily, toast, bacon and tea.

'I think I'm cured,' she said but carefully added: 'for the time being at any rate.' She was exuberant. She telephoned Kathleen in Scotland and told her how she felt. She wrote a six-page letter to her sister Eily and made plans to visit her in Ennis. She talked at length to me about taking a holiday together in Italy at Easter. She got up and came down to the fire by herself, played with the dogs, chatted for a long time with her friend Mary Heffernan. She was her old self again. (It was three o'clock on the afternoon of Tuesday, 9th February. On the following Tuesday, at three o'clock in the afternoon, the gravediggers were filling in her grave.) That night she told me not to bother reading to her as she wanted to sleep, and she felt I needed a good night's sleep too. I went to my room and lay down. I felt so happy; the worst was over and she was going to get better; I fell into a deep contented sleep.

On Wednesday morning, she was still in great form and ate a good breakfast. She was due to start another period of treatment at the clinic that afternoon, and she suggested that I should go into the office and catch up on the arrears of work, as young Mary, who had the afternoon off, could drive her to the clinic. I went to work with a light heart, deluding myself that she was on the mend.

I returned home shortly after six in the evening to find that she had had a complete relapse. She had not been to the clinic. She was too weak to go. She was out of pain, but was lifeless and listless. I stayed up with her all that night hoping that she would revive, but in the morning she was in a semi-coma. I woke her with some breakfast, but she barely touched it. Teresa MacSweeney called and washed her. Teresa was now alarmed and we sent for the family doctor. I stayed all the time in the room with Mary, holding her hand, and each time I asked her if she wanted anything, she replied faintly and without opening her eyes:

'No, Sean, I only want you. Stay with me. I love you.'

The family doctor came but there was little that could be done. Mary was dying fast.

I now sat constantly with her, holding her hand, caressing her hair, and gently sponging her face. When you sit for hours, holding the dying hand of someone you love, you seem to enter eternity, and in these moments life appears suddenly very different, and as you feel the throb of death beat faster and faster in the pulse you love, many of the things that you valued in this world seem futile and empty. In such a moment it becomes clear that the only reality in life is love, and I knew at that moment that death could not annihilate our love, however inadequately expressed on my part in the past.

As I sat there watching her life fade away my mind kept constantly turning back to the years of our youth together. I remembered Lahinch and the days of our young love, our marriage, our children as they came one by one, the founding of *The Mercier Press,* our struggles, our successes, our failures, the ups and downs that are the lot of all human life, the hopes, the joys, the friendships, the disappointments and the sorrows. In this mood I began to reflect on my own life and to wonder what I would do if I were to live it over again. I thought of J. M. Barrie's delightful play *Dear Brutus* where all the characters were given a second chance in life and how they made fools of themselves all over again. If I were given a second chance in life what would I do? Would I have stayed in the Army? Would I start *The Mercier Press?* Would I throw up everything and become a writer? Would I do the hundreds of things I thought I should have done? The answer to these questions was one vast fog of uncertainty. I just did not know. But in all this turmoil of doubt there was one unshakeable fact: *Given a second chance in life I would marry Mary again.* This was the one shining certainty in all the confusion of conjecture. Sitting there by her bedside, holding her hands in mine, I bent over her ear and said:

'Mary, if I had a thousand lives to live again I would love you and marry you a thousand times.'

But she did not hear. She was in a semi-coma, breathing the heavy breath of one about to die. Once again I was too late.

Later that day she came to, opened her eyes and said:

'Sean, darling, I want to be anointed.'

I knew she would like my brother James to annoint her, so I telephoned and asked him to come at once. He motored the seventy miles from Thurles in record time, and gave her absolution and anointed her. He had some doubts about whether she was able to take Holy Communion, and he expressed these aloud to Teresa, who was helping him. Mary heard him, immediately opened her eyes and spoke:

'I can take Holy Communion. I want it.'

He administered the Blessed Eucharist to her for the last time. He then prayed aloud:

O Lord Jesus Christ as we humbly stand in your presence, may the blessing of God, eternal happiness, peace and joy, living charity and everlasting health enter along with us. May the angels of peace make their dwelling here . . .

As he spoke the words 'everlasting health' a few tear-drops began to trickle from her eyes.

That night I stayed up with her again and about midnight she awoke screaming with a violent headache. She was twisting, turning, crying in agony. I gave her a special drug which the doctor said was only to be given in extreme pain; this eased her a lot and she slowly drifted back into the coma. Once again I asked her if she would like anything. Feebly she murmured:

'. . . only you, Sean . . . you are so good . . . you love me I know . . . I love you . . . I will always watch over you . . .' These were her last words on this earth.

The following day she was in an absolute coma. A doctor friend, Dr. George Rosenstock visited her, and he diagnosed pleurisy arising from secondary cancer. The family doctor was away so we sent for another doctor who was doing duty, and who very generously left a roomful of patients to come at once. She was sinking rapidly, but there was a hundred to one chance of her regaining consciousness and living a little longer if she could be got to hospital, her lungs tapped and the liquid drawn off. After several telephone calls he succeeded in getting her into St. Patrick's Hospital, Wellington Road, and, within minutes, the ambulance came and brought her away. She had left the home she loved for the last time.

Our usual specialist was away, but I managed to get another

who was kind enough to go to see her at once. He could not tap the lungs until the temperature dropped. He prescribed antibiotics to get the temperature down. Now we could only wait.

Late that night, James arrived with Kathleen. He had driven to Dublin airport to meet her, and immediately they arrived they went to St. Patrick's Hospital to see Mary. They came away with the feeling that she would not live the night. The temperature showed no signs of dropping.

All the family were now at home, and at varying times we went to see her over her last two days, but she never regained consciousness.

The last time I saw her I held her hand in mine for a long time. I bent over her and spoke into her ear:

'This is Sean. I love you, Mary. You will always be with me. I will never fail you.'

I felt the slightest pressure of her fingers on my hand, and the very faintest trace of an understanding smile on her lips.

Her temperature never dropped. The liquid could not be drawn off her lungs.

In the early hours of Monday morning, February 15th, 1971, while we were all sleeping at home, she died, alone.

Chapter Five

To love means to say: You will never die.

Gabriel Marcel

When the requiem mass ended, Mary's last long journey to her grave began. Dualla was sixty-five miles away. Our car, which Paudie drove, followed immediately behind the hearse, and I sat beside him in the front; Kathleen, Mary, and Gerald were in the back. Sean drove Mary's sister Eily and her young daughter in the car immediately following, while thirty or forty other cars made up the cortège and accompanied us to the graveyard.

As we drove through the city I was struck by the reaction of the people on the streets to death; a hearse, a coffin, flowers, mourners were a perfectly ordinary and frequent sight; the people looked, turned their heads quickly away, and went about their business. Death was not their affair and they did not want to be reminded of it. How bitter I felt towards them for their indifference, not bothering to remind myself that I, too, was equally indifferent when, in the past, I saw other funerals. As we moved through the familiar streets my desolation of spirit was beyond belief. How well I remembered them all. Together, we had walked and shopped and driven through them hundreds of times. Passing the clinic, where so much hope was raised and so much pain endured, I saw a man helping his young wife from a car and linking her, as she struggled painfully into the hall; their faces spoke of hope, just as ours had a few short weeks before. Across the river was the County Club where, in the months before her death, we had lunched together so often. As we slowly moved by *The Mercier Press* and the bookshop she founded, the whole of our lives flashed before me again. All at once, as in a montage, each scene dissolving into the other, I saw the hall in Lahinch and our first meeting, our young love together, our early married life, our growing children, our struggles, trials, and final success. I saw too the weak, wasted body of those last days. But it was all over now:

Ah Love! Could you and I with Him conspire
To grasp this sorry scheme of things entire
Would not we shatter it to bits—and then
Re-mould it nearer to the hearts desire.

At the end of McCurtain Street we passed the Windsor Hotel, where she stayed on her first visit to Cork in October 1944. It was here we had our wedding breakfast. There were six people at it, and it cost the princely sum of £7.10s. It was all she could afford. She was now leaving Cork by the same route she entered it twenty-six years before. She had arrived at Glanmire Road Station with two battered suitcases and £10 in her purse; of that, £7.10s was to pay for the wedding breakfast. With the change, she began her life with me.

Soon the hearse gathered speed as it left the city and moved through the countryside. How differently the country dweller saw death; as we passed, people stopped work; the men took off their hats and crossed themselves; the lips of the women moved in silent prayer. It seemed the people of the land, so close to nature, saw in death not something to be frightened of, but a reality to be reckoned with.

In the car we were silent; no one was inclined to speak. We seemed to have wanted to be alone with our thoughts and our memories of her. In front was a hearse, inside that hearse a coffin, and inside that coffin all that was left of a lifetime of goodness and love. That which made her Mary, which made her what she was, was gone from this earth and was now part of the eternal. Only the shell remained. I remember, at some time, saying to the children as we drove along:

'She is not out there. If she is anywhere, she is in the car with us.'

The silence in the car allowed me to think, to think about that remarkable human being who had shared my life. Why was it that she, so shy and retiring, made such an impact on people? Why did so many feel in her presence as if she were outside this world? Why was she so unselfish, gentle, calm, good, compassionate and kind? What made her radiate above all others? What really made her tick?

In trying to discover Mary's soul, I am limited by two factors. One: it is extremely difficult to examine and probe goodness in another person; one can only sense it and recognise it. Every human being is in some way a mystery to every other, even those we love. There are depths in each soul which are highly personal and where truth reigns in supreme silence, and one should not try to invade this privacy. Two: even if one could conceive in the mind what it is, human language is inadequate to describe it. Words can only produce images and goodness is not an image. In the months before her death she seemed to soar away beyond this earth, away beyond anything I was capable of following or understanding. All that I knew of the nobler things of life had come from books. Her knowledge had come from pure love of those things, and as I watched her in her last hours, when she was no longer able to speak, I learned, as if by grace, one profound lesson, which I hope has not come too late: *we do not get to know goodness by reading or talking about it; we get to know it by living it.* And this principle applies, not only to goodness, but to every other human virtue.

I had lived with her for twenty-six years in the closest relationship possible on this earth, and if anyone should know the answer to these questions I should; yet I am not sure. The deepest recesses of the human soul are known only to itself and to God and, the greater the soul, the less one can see. There were areas in Mary which will be for ever hidden, for ever obscured; other areas, I was permitted only occasional glances behind the veil that concealed her inner life.

From the moment she knew she was going to die she spoke more freely to me than ever before about life's fundamental experiences, death, suffering, disillusionment, hope, happiness and joy. In those long hours we spent together, with the shadow of death over her, either driving through the countryside, sailing the seas, or just sitting by our fireside, I succeeded in some small way in penetrating the veil and getting a fleeting glimpse of her beautiful soul. The great difficulty, however, was that her thoughts on these fundamental things were too deep and profound for me to grasp. What seemed a simple clear-cut issue to her, frightened me.

Mary's secret was that she was deeply religious. She was a believing and practising Catholic, and her life was motivated by the ideals of a true Christianity.

This statement needs a lot of explaining, since the Catholic Church shelters quite a few saints and an abnormally large number of scoundrels. The scoundrels are so adept at projecting themselves as saints, and the saints are so adept at self-effacement, that it is hard to distinguish between the two. Unlike the pre-conciliar narrow Irish Catholic, Mary could be described as an enlightened post-conciliar member of the Church.

A pre-conciliar Irish Catholic could be distinguished by a pre-occupation with non-essentials, and by what Cardinal Newman criticised as a 'lust for servility'. The external practices of the Church had pride of place; attendance at Mass, reception of the sacraments, membership of sodalities, participation in novenas, visits to shrines and, above all, generous cash contributions to every ecclesiastic who held out his hand, were the marks of a good Irish Catholic. Their religion was shallow and empty. They were great churchgoers, but any idea that the words of Christ should be taken literally would astonish and confuse them. Christ was carefully locked up in the tabernacle, surrounded by expensive ornaments, lamps and candles, and he was best left there. Add to that absolute blind obedience to all ecclesiastical superiors, however low their I.Q., acceptance of their opinions on almost all matters, but particularly on politics, education, and sex, and you had the Irish Catholic who was considered a certainty for the highest place in heaven. That these Catholics committed perjury in the courts, were dishonest in business, crushed their weaker brothers, were cruel and inhuman in personal relationships, disregarded truth when it suited them, was something that was quietly glossed over, or regarded with a shrug of the shoulders. Religion had become a form of insurance policy, where the individual paid a daily, weekly or monthly premium in the form of prayers, novenas and cash, and in return, would collect the capital sum, plus accumulated profits, in the next world. Like the Cabinet Minister, the T.D., or the County Councillor, God could be fixed. He had his price like everyone else. These people were the solid citizens, the ecclesiastical gombeen men of Ireland, respected by all. They drifted through their selfish lives with small, smug, miserable minds, confusing hypocritical Victorian practices with real Christian living. This mode of life was unfortunately condoned from many pulpits, giving them the necessary backing to wax fat in their egocentric beings, and to wallow in the moral cowardice which prevented them from thinking for themselves.

Mary's religion was diametrically opposed to this. The external practices of her faith she saw as the icing on the cake, but not the real nourishment; the blossom on the flower, which bloomed and died, but not the roots which lived on. She heard Mass regularly, daily where possible, but in her Mass, Christ was crucified again for the ideals, the way of life which He taught. Those ideals were meant to permeate our daily living and, after attending Mass, one should, she held, be a far better member of the Christian community in the widest human sense. The Mass was the core of her life, and she believed that if regular attendance at Mass did not produce profound changes for the better at all levels of personality, then there was something fundamentally and radically wrong.

She could see little point in the existence of sodalities, most of which she believed were founded by well meaning cranks and later exploited by their successors. As a young girl in the convent in Ennis, she was enrolled as a Child of Mary, and despite her doubts, she had a nostalgic affection for that organisation. I recall, on one occasion, she got a circular through the post, suggesting that she join one of those pious unions; the advantages looked quite attractive: a share in thousands of Masses, special blessings apparently not available to ordinary Catholics, a plenary indulgence at the hour of death, etc., etc. To stress what a popular society this was, its promoters emphasised that they had already half a million members. At the end of the document there was a detachable enrolment form, and one was asked to subscribe the small sum of five shillings per year to cover, what was described as, administrative and other costs. Mary did a quick calculation. Half a million five shillings came to £125,000. This was not a bad annual income, she thought, and one could understand the diligence of the promoters to get new members. Whenever she was asked by her friends to join one of these organisations she would say: 'Find me one that is not making money, and I will join it.'

She subscribed generously to the building of churches only when she was absolutely convinced that such building was necessary, but the mere fact that a cardinal or bishop said it was necessary would carry no weight with her. Here she always decided for herself, and if her decision was negative no human respect or moral pressure would influence her.

Her tremendous sense of reality bore the mark of greatness, and sometimes a touch of stringent humour crept in. An example of this was her attitude to the problem of prostitution in Cork. She felt that the establishment by the Church authorities of a social club for sailors, as a solution to this problem, was typical of the muddled and weak-minded thinking which had done such incalculable damage to the Catholic Church. She knew that a club for sailors would have absolutely no effect on the lessening of prostitution on the quays. When the club closed at 11.30 at night she knew what some of the sailors, on their way back to the ships, would go looking for—and it was not someone to answer the rosary! She refused to give any financial help to this club, but she was prepared to give substantial financial help if the Church authorities would face reality, and establish a regular brothel on the quays; a properly supervised brothel, with ten or twelve girls, would mean the end of sixty or seventy amateur prostitutes in the city. I need hardly say that her suggestions were not too well received. Nevertheless the club became a reality, it has many excellent amenities for the regular flow of foreign sailors through the port, and it has done quite a lot of helpful work. On the other hand, prostitution is flourishing as much as ever on the quays.

But all these things were merely the unimportant externals, and her attitude towards them simply indicates the clear thinking, the deep mature religion, and the moral courage of one who tried to live constantly with God. In a way, she stands at the cross roads between the old Irish heresies and the awakening of real true Christianity in the nation, and she was not alone in this. To grasp, however, the inner Mary is not as simple as to describe her outward reactions, but I can from what I saw, and from what she spoke about, give some idea, however imperfect, of what that was like.

A vital principle which motivated her life was the complete acceptance of what she believed to be the universal law. The universal law was the law of the Creator and was inherent in the creation of the universe; it was there from the beginning of time and it was unchangeable; it was an inexplicable law and it brought with it far more suffering than joy; it was the law of our imperfect world moving towards fulfilment. This universal law embodied her saying 'yes' to life, and it followed that she said 'yes' also to the sorrows and sufferings of life. Evils, such as physical and mental pain, frustrations, disappointments, mistakes, betrayals, as well as the joys and contentments of life, were all part of this inflexible law, and one either accepted or rejected it. The logical consequence of rejection was suicide: the logical consequence of acceptance was fulfilment in life. But these are extremes, and most people did not go to extremes but gave it a partial acceptance, a partial rejection, or what was indeed much more common, a running away from it through selfishness, drink, drugs, bad temper and even through religion itself. One practical consequence of Mary's acceptance of this law was that, unlike so many, she did not pray for material or physical gain, because she believed that, in doing so, she was asking the Creator to set aside the universal law for her special benefit, and not alone was this asking for a miracle, but it was projecting herself above everyone else as someone upon whom God should bestow special favours. Of course she was regularly faced with the words of Christ, *ask and you shall receive,* but she understood those words to mean: *do not ask for a change, but ask for the strength and grace to accept and face up to the realities of the universal law, and if you do, this strength will be given to you, as it will be given to all who ask, without exception.* Mary did not pray to be relieved of her cancer pains, but she did pray to get the strength to face them and not to let them defeat her; on the other hand, she took the drugs prescribed by the doctors to ease the pains, because these drugs, and the whole healing process of medicine, emerged from and was part of the universal law. She did not pray for the success of her business ventures; instead, she applied her whole being to the task on hand, and used to the full the brain and ability God gave her. She did, however, pray for the strength to do this, and for the strength to face the difficulties which she met daily. What she prayed for under the exhortation *ask and you shall receive* was for an inner strength; and as far as we humans can judge, her prayers were answered.

She saw that if she were to give any meaning to her life she would have to lift herself above temporal things and eternalise them. She was unable to influence world events, or indeed most of the local events of her daily life, but by lifting them on to the spiritual level she was able to meet them head on, however painful, and deal with them. She had accepted the fact that everything that is beautiful in this world is in some way or another united to that which is ugly and often and often she pondered Goethe's terrible question: *Must the things that make a human being happy in this world, ultimately become the source of his misery and unhappiness?* In her life she experienced this over and over again, but she had such reserves of inner strength that she could uplift everything and make it part of the eternal. This may be one explanation for her absolute calmness in the face of adversity.

Another part of the consequence of her acceptance of this universal law was that she saw her life on earth as part of eternity. They were not two separate existences; one was a continuation of the other on a far higher level. She saw in death the abandoning of the body, as the butterfly abandons the cocoon in which it has grown and developed during its time of chrysalis. The human body was really only the 'womb' in which an infinite spirit developed and formed during a lifetime. The role of the womb ends at birth, so the role of the body ends at death, when the infinite spirit enters the totality of being. She saw human life as being in the womb of time, and through death it burst forth into eternity. She believed that our state in eternity depended entirely on the way we fulfilled our role in the world of time. She saw our role in this life not as a continuous series of individual actions, but as an attitude which inspired and motivated our relationship to others, to ourselves, to animals, to plants, indeed to every form of creation. She believed that every action of ours, in this role in life, was either an action which united us with God in the eternal or which separated us from him. Her test was as follows: If the action was motivated by selfishness, then it was a separating action; if it was motivated by the unselfish application of the ideals of truth, justice, and charity, then it was a unifying action. After death, each individual is what he has become, through his various actions and decisions, and if they have been unselfish then total fulfilment in unity with God follows; if they have been selfish then total suffering, or perhaps total annihilation, follows.

These beliefs of hers seem simple on the surface but their

practical application to daily life was very far-reaching and very difficult. According to these principles, a Catholic who attended Mass, sacraments, and all other religious duties regularly and who, before death, even received the last sacraments, could quite easily be separated for all eternity from God. If such a person's religious actions were motivated by selfishness, then these actions were even worse than useless. By selfishness she meant self-adoration, trying to fix our place in the next world, trying to save our skin in eternity, to 'square' God. Only the very purest motives of unselfish love of God gave religious action or formulas any meaning.

Her religion was centred on Christ. She believed that He was wholly God and wholly human, and if she were to become one with God, then she would have to become, like Christ, wholly human too. She would have to open herself up to others and only by doing so could she open herself completely to God. The way to God lay through the thorny paths of other peoples lives. She did not divide people into those she liked and those she disliked; she gave herself without reserve to all. She saw in every human being a person who had the right to life, who had the right to be what they were and she met them as such, with respect, honesty, patience, and understanding. Of course she was let down time and time again by those she helped and trusted, but she accepted these betrayals as a normal part of living and did not become hard or embittered, but continued on with a magnanimous trust in the ultimate goodness hidden in every human being.

Most suffering in the world she saw as the direct result of human greed, beginning with the individual and ending with nations; *I want what you have, whether it be your money, your wife, your husband, your job, your prospects, your peace, your intelligence, and indeed, in the end, your country.*

Physical suffering and pain she found hard to rationalise,

hard to explain. She accepted it as part of the universal law but she freely admitted that she could not understand why God permitted so much of what to the human mind seemed so utterly senseless.

To face life in this way meant that she had detached herself from temporal things while still being fully involved in them. If death is the complete destruction of all temporal things, then death had nothing to take from her for she had already transcended what death could take. This may help to explain why she was not afraid to die.

If the motives of her daily living were the noblest and the highest possible, then this gives a clue to her impact on people. Goodness just radiates from one who is wholly good, and its magnetism touches all who come in contact with it. Her life, allowing for human frailty, was goodness itself. She had found a meaning for life from which a strange, helpful power seemed to overflow. Those who met her recognised and felt this but could not explain it; to many she was an enigma, but an enigma that made them feel better and happier for knowing her, which in the last analysis is the final product of a total unselfishness. For most of us in this world, the future means money, fame and success; for her the future was a place called heaven.

Mary led a simple, retiring, obscure life, moving through our midst softly and noiselessly, and now all that was left of her was passing quietly on its way to the grave. But this was not the end. Human beings die, but goodness lives on. Her goodness did not die with her. It lives on in a quiet way through all those to whom she brought peace and joy and fulfilment, through the poor, the underprivileged, the sick, the old, the mentally tormented, the many physical and spiritual wrecks she met and helped throughout her life. As I travelled behind the hearse on that cold February day, with all these thoughts in my mind, it slowly began to penetrate my dull, stupid brain that I had been loved by, and married to, a saint of the modern world—and I had not even known it.

*

Dearest Mary: Yesterday I had a long talk with Patrick C. Power, and together we recalled his visit to you about a month before you died. He had just completed a new translation of The Midnight Court *by Brian Merriman, and he wanted to check some of the local Clare place-names with you. Afterwards he told you about a special kind of apple-wine he had made, and he would send you some of it in March. Very sadly you told him that you would not be there in March.*

'You must fight Mary. You must fight,' Pat said.

'My fighting days are over,' you answered quietly. 'The end is almost here.'

Pat was astounded at your calm serene attitude, devoid of fear or terror. A month later, after attending your funeral in Dualla, he drove home silently, filled with sadness. Once inside his house, he sat down and wrote a poem for you; here it is as he wrote it, without change:

Funeral at Dualla

The black wall, the end,
The sun sickly,
The day of turned clay
The end of the journey.

The black wall, the cloud;
The hand-clasping;
The coffin shouts to the sky
The end of the journey.

The black wall, the words;
The murmuring;
The smiles that freeze the air;
The end of the journey.

The black wall, the start;
The departure;
The going faraway
To begin a journey.

For dear Mary. Patrick C. Power

★

Passing through Cashel, the hearse slowed down to allow ten or twelve waiting cars to join the cortège, and then began the short three-mile journey to Dualla. The road from Cashel climbs steadily up a long incline, known as the Mile Hill, and then makes a sharper descent into the little village. When we reached the top, the whole panorama of the valley spread out before us. Away to the south, Slievenamon, where we had our cottage, set against the blue background of the Knockmealdown mountains; to the east the furze-covered Kill Hills, and to the north the green luxuriant slopes of Mount O'Meara. These were the hills that had encircled all my youth. Straight ahead, at the end of the valley, was Dualla church and beside it the little graveyard. My heart began to pound, and as we came nearer there was a hammering at my temples and a buzzing in my ears. The end of a lifetime was in sight.

The road outside the graveyard was lined on both sides with cars of people who came from Dublin, Galway, Kerry, Limerick, Waterford, and other parts of the country. A large crowd, many of whom I had not seen since childhood, had gathered in the graveyard. Mary's coffin was shouldered by her two sons Gerald and Sean; with two friends, they carried it to the graveside. Her brothers Sean and Pat, her sister Eily, the four children and myself stood by the edge of the grave. It looked so deep and frightening. The crowd closed in when my brother James began to recite the prayers:

> *O God of mercy and compassion we humbly ask you to be mindful of your servant Mary whom you have now called from this life. Bring her to her true home in heaven; that, as she believed and hoped, she may enjoy everlasting happiness.*

As James was praying I could see her again, as I saw her long ago, with the Atlantic wind blowing her dark young hair across her face. I could see her sallow skin radiant, her brown eyes, her face without a wrinkle.

The crowd had pressed close around the grave, their heads lowered, their faces grim and drawn. I should have been praying, but my heart and soul were numb. I looked up from the coffin and saw in the distance the face of Mary Keane. Tears were welling in her eyes. I do not know why she should, at that terrible moment in my life, remind me of a beautiful poem her husband John B. Keane, the dramatist, had written for her years before, when he was going away from her for the first time:

O my love, my own love, lie down here beside me,
O my love, my dear love, O sweet love betide me,
Lie still in my arms, do not moan, love, or tremble,
The wild doves are sleeping high on the green bramble.

James continued praying:

Show your mercy to your servant Mary who has departed this life, that as she was numbered among the faithful on earth she may be brought into the company of your angels in heaven.

The coffin was lowered on ropes, deep down into the grave. The words of Keane's poem still kept haunting my mind:

All over Feale river the shadows are falling,
And deep in Shanowen the vixen is calling,
The sweet night is young, love, the night is for ever,
And shadows are falling all over Feale river.

Standing by the open grave, strange tangled memories of the past rushed wildly through my head. I remembered a holiday I had spent with her in the North Kerry country at the suggestion of John B. Arm in arm we had rambled together along the banks of the Feale river. We watched the salmon jumping in the pools. We listened to the wild and lonely call of the curlews returning to the sedgy banks. We had bathed and swum in the breaking surf at Ballybunion. In the evening we strolled along the cliffs, watching the young lovers beginning their lives together, as we had done so many years before. Sometimes in the late summer evenings we climbed the side of Knockanore mountain. To the south we could see the vast panorama of headlands and islands lit by the slanting sun: Kerry Head, Mount Brandon, The Three Sisters, The Great

Blasket, Inisvickallane and Inis na mBro. Across the lordly Shannon we could see her homeland, and the hills of Clare.

I would fly like a bird with white wings in the air
Or swim the wild waters far off into Clare
The sweet night is young, love, the night is forever
And shadows are falling all over Feale river.

Another priest, Father John O'Dwyer, said aloud the customary prayer for the mourners:

O Lord Jesus Christ, God of all consolation, whose heart was moved to tears at the grave of Lazarus, look now with compassion on your servants who are sorely grieved by their loss. Strengthen in their hearts the spirit of faith to accept this cross from your loving hands. Give to their troubled hearts, and to the hearts of all men the light of hope, that they may so live as one day to be united again where all tears shall be wiped away in the kingdom of your love.

The gravediggers got ready for their grim task. A stifled sob could be heard here and there in the crowd. Somewhere in the distance the rich, triumphant voice of a lark soared upwards through the still clear air. Spring was back 'with rustling shade, and apple blossoms filled the air'. Mary had not failed her rendezvous.

Soon, brown earth and rock and stone would cover the frail and wasted body of the woman I loved, and would for ever unite her to all that remained of the other woman closest to me in life, the woman at whose knees I learned to pray. The crowd would leave the graveyard having done their duty and paid their respects. Darkness would fall and everything would be silent and still. In a few weeks, or a few months, Mary would be forgotten by all, except by those whose bruised hearts now ached, and who would yearn for her in the long lonely nights of future years. Such is the law of life, her universal law, to be born, to live, to suffer, to die, to be forgotten. The only permanence is the permanence of change.

But there is always Hope. The hope . . . *to be united again where all tears shall be wiped away in the kingdom of your love . . .*

Chapter Six

Naked I wait thy loves' uplifted stroke!
My harness piece by piece thou hast hewn from me
And smitten me to my knee;
I am defenceless utterly.
I slept, methinks, and woke,
And, slowly gazing, find me stripped in sleep.
In the rash lustihead of my young powers,
I shook the pillaring hours
And pulled my life upon me; grimed with smears,
I stand amid the dust of the mounded years—
My mangled youth lies dead beneath the heap
My days have crackled and gone up in smoke,
Have puffed and burst as sun-starts on a stream.

Francis Thompson

Relatives and friends form a kind of unity and protection during the sad days of a funeral, but life must go on and, one by one, they leave; they have their own world and their own problems, and their own lives to face. Then one is alone.

Waking up the morning after Mary's burial was a strange and confusing experience. I had taken a mild sedative before going to bed and had slept reasonably well. I came downstairs and sat in the breakfast room staring out the window; I was staring at nothing, thinking of nothing, perceiving nothing;

I was lost in a kind of an intellectual fog, with only the odd glimpse of reality coming through. I felt I should do something, but what I should do I did not know, and even if I did, I was so mentally paralysed that I just could not do it. The earth, the sky, the familiar world outside my window was gone out of focus, and even daydreaming was something beyond me. I was gripped with an unusual fear because I did not know what to expect; nor did I really know what I was afraid of. Perhaps, I thought, it was the loveless, companionless, empty unknown, the terrible, unreachable distance of Mary away from me? I sat there for more than an hour with confused thoughts, a stranger to myself, lost and bewildered in a world that had become uninhabitable for me. Later Kathleen came down and began to get the breakfast, and soon we were joined by the other children, and we tried to talk in a normal way, as if nothing had happened. But there were long pauses and long silences and long periods of emptiness. We had entered the first phase of grief, the easiest phase because of its closeness to the event, and because of the practical things that had to be seen to immediately, and also because the realisation that Mary would never come back had not fully dawned on us. There was a second, and more excruciating, phase to come.

The first phase lasted little over two weeks, and then I began to be aware that I was slowly entering the strange and bewildering world of sorrow, a world with no boundaries, a world of pain-filled days and dark, starless nights. It was a world I did not know but which seemed to vary in intensity and to have no fixed standards other than those of pain and desolation. Not that sorrow, pain, disappointment, disillusionment were new to me—indeed they were old acquaintances—but I now felt that they would take up permanent abode and remain with me to the end of my days. Every day seemed so completely unfamiliar. Existence itself felt shattered and unreal. I was on the outside of something, I did not know what, and I was adrift from life, like a ship left stranded by the ebbing tide.

The normal interests of full living, such as politics, world affairs, wars, television, radio, became something of no importance, and I could not now understand how they had ever meant anything to me. How could I think of the futile trappings of life when life itself had left me, and when all I wanted was to die and to be absorbed forever with Mary in Dualla? As time went on, I began to accept this completely unreal state as a state of normality, and this naturally affected my whole life and gave me a twisted and warped view of the world. There was now only one reality, the dead Mary in Dualla. This was the focal point of my life and nothing else mattered. Other people were mere shadowy forms to me and I treated them as such; how hurtful, unpleasant, and horrible I was, even to my family and to those close to me. In my stupidity I could not see that the one certain way to alienate myself from Mary was to do just what I was doing.

At work I would sit at my desk and try to deal with manuscripts, with letters, with problems, with people; but when I thought I was doing fine, I would suddenly remember her, and a jab of pain would pierce me through, and everything and everybody would seem futile again. I recall one of the most painful moments of all, when ordering a reprint of our note-paper heading, I had to strike out her name from the list of directors, and as I drew the pen through it, it was as if I were cutting my own soul in two.

But despite this traumatic state, the publishing programme of *The Mercier Press* went on, through the work of the wonderful staff, particularly Michael Roberts, John Spillane, Leonore Sierigk, Loretto MacNamara, and, in the Dublin office, Bernie Power. With a rare sympathy and understanding, they kept the organisation going and troubled me as little as possible;

they were reliable, dependable, and loyal. I left the office at odd and varying hours and walked home; I looked through the human beings I saw with a hatred and contempt; they were alive and Mary was dead. How could they mow their lawns, cut their hedges, sweep their footpaths, laugh and talk, when Mary was no more? On my way home I began to make detours to many of our favourite places; the table in the café where we sat together, our first flat, the church we attended in our youth, our favourite walks along the Mardyke, the street stalls, the antique shop, the hospital where she suffered and endured so much pain. One day I even went to St. Patrick's Hospital, and stole up to the ward window, from where I could see the bed in which she died; these and many other familiar places, each one giving the knife that extra painful twist in my heart. And then when I reached home the emptiness and silence were unnerving; everything was in its place and looked as if she would walk in from town any moment and greet me with a gentle smile. I sat aimlessly staring into space, listening to every sound, endlessly smoking cigarettes. Sometimes I would listen to music, but every wave of melody brought her back to me again. Other times I would go through her album of photographs and look at her pictures; as an infant, a smiling child, a young girl, a mother playing with our children, and then I would slow down and linger on the last photographs taken shortly before she died, her brave, noble face, still strikingly beautiful; and when I came to the last photograph of all, taken at Kathleen's wedding, just before she died, laughing happily with a glass of champagne in her hand, I would burst hopelessly and helplessly into tears. Often I'd get up and go out on the lawn and walk up and down, up and down, the narrow path, not knowing what to do or where to go, and in this way, I would brood alone until Sean and Mary returned late in the evening.

Sometimes the long hours at night, those hours of eerie silence and loneliness that no man can escape, almost broke my spirit. I re-read her favourite books; I recited in a low voice her best loved poems; I got up and worked hour after hour writing this book, painfully reliving it all again, until tiredness overcame me, and I wearily lay down to sleep, only to waken suddenly in the midst of a dream that she was alive again, speaking to me, helping me, filling my life with her presence; and then I would wake to the terrible reality; it was just a dream.

My suffering was not only mental; it was physical too. I developed pains in the pit of my stomach, a kind of contraction of the chest, and sometimes a phase of semi-blindness; headaches came and went with regularity, but the doctors rightly told me that they were psychological and that they could do nothing for me.

I tried to distract myself by going to parties and functions, but this did not help very much. Everywhere in the crowd, I saw her face, and if I did speak, invariably I found myself speaking of her, and as the party gathered strength, and the music became louder, I could see, in the midst of all the gaiety, her lonely grave in Dualla, and I would have the horrible wish that everyone in the room, now laughing and enjoying life, would soon die and find themselves buried for ever in the deep earth.

The grief came in waves, taking ghoulish and weird forms. Sometimes it came in the form of hate; I hated myself for all the wrongs I believed I had done her: I hated myself for the time and the joy I gave to others and which I should have given to her; I hated the doctors who did not save her; I even hated God for taking her from me: but the most vicious hate of all was directed towards anyone I thought had come between us, or kept me from her, or hurt her. I was twisted, confused, unbalanced, unsure of myself. Every day I had a new and more stupid plan for my life: I was going to enter a monastery; I was going to pack up everything and go on the missions; I was going to go to the Himalayas and live the life of a hermit; I even discussed the possibility of becoming a monk with a high-up ecclesiastic, who very properly just burst out laughing at me. Yet all the time, day in day out, sorrow gnawed at my heart, and sometimes, when I thought I had a little control over myself, my soul would suddenly send up a cry of despair which shook my very life to its foundation. It was a living hell.

But behind every dark cloud there is a tiny ray of sunshine. As a schoolchild I learned a poem beginning with the words: 'Laugh and the world laughs with you. Weep and you weep alone.' But I had not to weep entirely alone. In the midst of all this misery and suffering I had the loyalty and devotion of a few dear friends. As well as the members of my family and relatives, these few friends comforted me in every way. As the evenings grew longer, Leonore came and took me for drives in the country in her car; sometimes we stopped at the state forests and went for long walks with the dogs through the woodland paths. She sensed my gloomy, sullen mood, and she talked only when she felt I could respond. Later, she taught me how to play chess, and the many hours of silent concentration playing this marvellous game with her helped me to forget myself. The Hon. April and Quentin Agnew-Somerville placed their beautiful home in the County Meath at my disposal, and there for days at a time I wandered through the historic Boyne Valley and returned to a friendship and warmth which eased my worst pain. In Dublin, Maire O'Donnell was a true and gracious friend. We dined often together, and she, who knew Mary so intimately, listened with a rare sympathy as I read extracts from this book and poured out my sorrows; with Maire I began to regain the gift of joyous, happy laughter once again, and to rediscover my lost sense of humour. How delightful were the evenings I spent with Irene Comerford and Loretto MacNamara. Sometimes they came to the house, and together sang virtually every song I could request; other times we went to a pub, and under the releasing influence of the drop of drink, heated discussions took me out of myself, but soon we were all three singing happily again. In those bitter days I learned that one of the greatest gifts of any human being to another is the gift of trusting and loyal friendship.

There is a point reached when a man hits the bottom of the deep pit of suffering and can fall no further, and I had now reached that point, the point where, it seemed, only suicide and death could give me fulfilment. One day as I was driving aimlessly through the countryside, I found myself, quite accidentally, on the road to Cashel. It was the road of Mary's funeral and I slowed down and drove sorrowfully along the sad route, when suddenly the thought came to my mind to continue to Dualla. This gave me an empty, cowardly, sinking feeling but it also had a sobering effect. I had not been to her grave since the day they buried her and, that day, I was surrounded by friends and sympathisers; now I would be alone. How would I react standing by her grave in the loneliness of the little churchyard? My intellect urged me on, but my emotions were holding me back, and in the end the intellect won and I kept going.

As I drew nearer to Dualla, I became more and more uneasy; I felt sick and weak; I opened the window of the car to let in the air; I shut off the heat. I wanted to turn around and drive away but I did not seem to have the power to do so. Just outside the little village there is a roadsign with the printed word DUALLA and when I came to this, it seemed as if it were jumping up and down in its frame. I came to a halt and parked the car outside the gate. It was a grey still day in March. Hardly a sound could be heard. The mound of clay which was her grave was partly covered with the remains of garlands of flowers; they were withered, rotting, and decaying. Dear God! It was so hard to believe that her beautiful frail body was six feet under this heap of earth. This was my most painful moment, a moment of absolute, indescribable desolation, when human language reaches the bitter end. I had only one wish, one longing, which I spoke to her from my heart. *Mary, I want to die this moment and to be buried with you for ever. Please take me.*

I was not dramatic or hysterical. I meant every word I spoke, and this made me feel a little better. I felt a strange sickness inside me and, for a second, I thought my request would be granted. Then a peculiar thing happened. I thought she spoke to me. I did not hear her voice through my ears, but I heard it clearly in my soul: *You coward! Why are you wallowing in your own self-pity. You are too full of self-love to face the realities of life and to live it fully and completely as you should. I have faced death, which is the loneliest and most painful experience of all. I cannot be with you if you are a coward. Pull yourself together and be a man; the man I always believed you were; the man I loved more than life itself!*

Cold sweat began to break out all over me. I was stunned and dizzy, and nearly fell backwards on the brown earth. In a kind of a daze I found my way into the church and sat down in front of the altar. It was not the first time that I had sat there with a sad and aching heart. As a little boy, suffering the terrible unhappiness and loneliness of being without a mother, I had often stolen out from home, ran all the way to my mother's grave, sat and cried in the little church, until I had no more tears to shed; and now after forty years I was back again in the same seat, before the same altar, and with the same loneliness in my heart.

Slowly, bit by bit my thinking processes came back to life. I suppose we all find it hard to look honestly at ourselves, to stand far enough away and not become dazzled by the wonderful person we think we are. In the stillness of the church, I began to take a hard look at myself, not at the person I thought I was, but the person I really was. I had betrayed her badly, wrapped up in my self-importance and in the search for comfort and consolation, and I knew that if she were in my place, she would not try to minimise her pain, but she would try to build up her resources and to steel her spirit to the task of living. Her prayer would not be a cowardly wail for consolation, but a noble call for the strength to face a new and harder world.

There have been times in my life when, as it were, the scales of blindness fell suddenly from my eyes, and I saw things which were obvious to everyone except myself, in the full light of reality. This was one of those moments, and I saw that in our life together I was the failure, she was the success. So many of my friends had told me, to my face, that she was far too good for me. Now I saw how right they were.

Almost unknown to myself, I began to probe deeply into the dark hidden depths of my own soul; to examine those forces in me which had motivated my life, and which had brought with them so much good on the one hand and so much more evil on the other. I was her superior in those things which were empty and unimportant and shallow: money-making, business affairs, social life, high sounding conversation, fame, material achievements. She was my superior, so far above me in everything that was really important in life: goodness, understanding, humility, loyalty, kindness, and love. I was one of those people who thought, because of the work I was doing, that I was somebody great, somebody important, somebody indispensable, and I acted in a way befitting this exalted opinion of myself. I could hold an audience spellbound in conversation, making the most intelligent remarks and the most penetrating observations in such a way that I exercised a great attraction for people, and even moved their hearts. They sought me out, cultivated me, and invited me to their gatherings, where I became the centre of attraction, the great showpiece, the intellectual poltergeist. I now saw how empty and shallow and meaningless all this was. My tongue spoke, and every trashy word I uttered was in reality turning back on me and poisoning my real self, which Mary so much wanted to nourish. I was the performer who performed, not to help people, to bring them joy, comfort, or even enlightenment, but to satisfy my own pride, and to put myself in the centre of the world. Mary, on the other hand, never tried to make herself greater than she was. There was no split or division between what she said and what she did. Silent, self-effacing, retiring, she poured out kindness on everyone that came her way, never expecting anything in return, never seeking the praise or acclamation of the crowd, satisfied and happy that she had brought a few moments of joy to somebody who needed it. She let her life and her actions speak for her, while I let empty meaningless words and phrases speak for me. I had failed to translate my knowledge into meaningful, outgoing experience, I had failed to make it a genuine reality, and I could only talk about it in terms which in the end meant nothing. She was what she wished others to become, while I just preached and lectured.

It is a strange thing that in those rare moments of self-illumination which come upon us, how really truthful to ourselves we can be. Once we decide to strip ourselves of the bluff, to stop throwing dust in our own eyes, it seems as if the deepest recesses of the soul open up to receive the full, painful, blinding flashes of Truth. As I sat there alone in the little church, with only the ticking of the clock breaking the silence, I watched the steady, constant, ever-burning flame of the sanctuary lamp and it seemed to symbolise for me the whole idea of love, and I began to grasp and experience in a very intense way what Mary's love for me really meant,

It was a love which put me above herself, a kind of an emptying of her own self so that my life could fill the space which was left. She loved me as I was with all my failings, my self-centredness, my indifference, my moodiness, my restlessness, and sought nothing in return; it was pure and unselfish. She stood by me and supported me, even though at times this demanded a blind act of confidence on her part, and I knew with absolute certainty that I could depend totally and completely upon her in all situations, however much I had hurt her or let her down. She compiled no catalogue of my failings and weaknesses to throw back in my face at the first suitable opportunity, but gently and kindly forgave all and forgot all.

She once said to me that *to love is to know* but *to know is not necessarily to love;* I had not really understood what she meant, but now it was becoming clear to me. In the first place, she loved God with her whole being; she knew and understood Him in a way that I could never grasp; she loved life and every living thing; she loved me with every fibre and she knew me through and through; her love was far too deep to be blind. Hundreds of parts of a jigsaw now began to fall into place. I saw how I had let her down so often, and wounded her in so many ways. I had failed hopelessly to distinguish the gold from the dirt, and because she had never spoken about the many stupid mistakes I made, I thought she was unaware of them—but I was wrong as usual, and had once again underestimated her. Her good taste, her dignity, soared upwards into a silence that was the essence of an understanding and a trust which instinctively told her that, however misled I was, I would not make the final idiotic blunders that could destroy anything good and noble in my life. Truth, as she said, would always win the last battle, and time has proven this judgement correct.

I now realised that a new moment of truth had arrived in my life. I had known and loved her as she was, in the spatio-temporal condition of this world, but I was now to know and love her far more intensely and deeply in the conditions of the spirit and in the context of eternity. But I knew, if I were to start living life again, it would have to be based on absolutes, and my most secret thoughts would be an open book to hre; she would see everything in one moment of vision, in one flash. I would have to live life on the level of reality, and only Truth could now be the final standard.

I had spent more than an hour in the church, an hour of painful soul-searching, in which I had seen the abysmal self-delusion of my own life and I had recoiled in horror. But despite all this, or perhaps as a result of it, I came up with a very rough philosophy of living, hastily put together, which I could see might fulfil my life and, at the same time, unite me, as close as my spatio-temporal state would allow, to the spirit of the woman I loved. I would try to adopt her great virtues, unselfishness, goodness, courage, reverence for life, as my future ideals. Translated into reality, this meant that I should try to fulfil these virtues as she did, in every thought, word, or action, irrespective of the person, place, or circumstances involved. The practical application of this was, and is, proving back-breaking to one who had lived most of his life with phoney standards. I now would have to begin the journey over the longest and hardest of all roads, the road back to life, the road back to my true self. My hoodwinking days were over.

It was almost dark when I left the little church, and in the twilight I bent over her grave and thanked her in words that surged from my soul. I was calm at last. My heart was light and happy. It was as if we had been married again and I was getting a second chance. The journey back to Cork was one of cheerfulness and joy; the gloom of desolation had left me, and now and then I found myself whistling the air of a lively song.

At home I sat down in my study and became very practical and I made a plan. I laid down attainable objectives in my work for a six months' period, and I laid down similar objectives in my personal life, and I determined, whatever happened, to follow these through. But the key to all this was to face a full life, inspired by her courage and bravery, in a way that would enable me to come to final victory over the self-delusion that was my world. I had now accepted that death was not the end, but in a more realistic way it was the beginning.

Because of this, I became rather curious about death and the dead, and I read all I could lay my hands on about this subject, and discussed it with people I felt should know, and gradually I began to understand a little; I began to see the dead in a rather different light, and to see them as so superior to us in every way that it is they who must surely pity us. A graveyard no longer became for me a place of gloom, but a place almost of envy; a place where sorrow and despair and suffering ended and real life began. Beyond the grave there are no croziers, no crowns, no medals, no decorations, no Mercedes. We will hold in our hands only what we were in life, only our unselfishness, our generosity, our sacrifices, and our love.

One day that Spring, when all nature was bursting into life, I was strolling through the fields near Dualla, in a state of semi-joy, semi-sorrow, when I saw a sight which was both frightening and profound. A sheep, lying on its side in the open grass, was giving birth to a lamb; it seemed a painful and a hard birth. The little lamb was only partly out of its mother's womb when it was attacked by a flock of ravens, and before I got to the scene and really saw what was happening, the ravens had torn the lamb's eyes out and ripped large gashes in its frail body. The mother, in the pangs of birth-pain, was bleating pitifully but could do nothing, and in a few minutes the lamb was dead, while not yet fully born. As I went away, the ravens returned, and set about finishing their grim meal. The whole scene was a nauseating sight, and I left it with disgust.

As I strolled along in a meditative, but disturbed mood, it seemed to me that we humans do not act very differently from the ravens. We admire the frolicking lamb as we pass, and even may write poetry about it, but we still slaughter and eat it like the ravens. Was there much difference between the scene I just witnessed and any butcher's slaughterhouse? The ravens tore the flesh to pieces and gobbled it down to nourish themselves and to live. We present the little lamb's flesh on a beautiful dish, covered with sauces, but its final fate is just the same; we are simply that little bit more sophisticated. Like other imperfect forms of life on this earth, we live entirely off death and destruction; the death of something gives us what we eat; the death of something else gives us what we wear; death simply regulates our whole existence. It is death which makes all things live and in another way it is life which makes all things die. Inside our own bodies, thousands of microbes are fighting it out to destruction at any given moment; we have only to look closely at the most beautiful landscape on a summer's day to find that, under every tuft of grass, this mass slaughter is taking place; under the deep blue sea hundreds of thousands of creatures are tearing each other to pieces in a carnage greater than anything on land. It is an unpleasant fact, but one which must be faced, that our being alive depends entirely on how efficiently, and in many cases how cruelly, we can destroy other forms of life. This human body of ours which we adore, and which we try to beautify so much, can only be what it is through the destruction and death of other forms of created life—forms as beautiful, in their own ways, as ours.

As I lay in the long grass, brooding on these unpleasant facts, it seemed to me that the dead are free of all this; for them it is over. They no longer depend for their existence on destruction; they exist in one complete act of love without any trimmings. Their intellects alone are so powerful that they see all the mysteries of life in one vision, with no human dung-hill intervening. They know the answers to every baffling question; they know the last unwritten and revealing chapter in the book of life. Compared to us, they are so far superior in beauty and intelligence as to defy understanding by the weak human brain. But what is of far greater importance is, as Frank Sheed says: 'They are more closely united to us now than in any closeness known upon earth.' The love which they bear us is a completely purified form of love, devoid of all selfishness and possessiveness; it is a burning flame millions of times more intense than ever earthly love could be.

If these conclusions were right, and I have no reason to believe they were not, then Mary loved me with an intensity unknown on this earth; she was also infinitely closer to me than when she was alive. This thought alone made the task of facing life again much more fulfilling, and purposeful. It seemed almost necessary for her to die that I might discover the truth and reality of life. It seemed, also, that if I wanted to pierce through to her from my side, the only way was to pierce through life itself, and that meant living to the full every moment of every day, not running away from or avoiding the problems that faced me, trying to make sure that only the highest ideals motivated every action. To participate in this life, I would have to regularly take the measure of my own faults, and clearly see my own nothingness especially when I felt inclined to slip. Truth would have to become the centre of life, all action would have to become in some way, however imperfect, part of the eternal. This world, so familiar to her when she lived, would be so strange to me; it was a world of unselfishness, of purity of intention; a world where one lived outside oneself, where selfishness and egoism were the ultimate evils. Indeed the atmosphere of this world was so rarefied and sharp as to overwhelm one who was used to the stinking atmosphere of self; it is only bit by bit I am coming to understand it.

*

Dearest Mary: I am coming to the end of this book and I have my great doubts whether it would please you or not. It comes from what is deepest in me and I simply had to write it. There are things in life, good and bad, pleasurable and painful, that we have to do, whatever the consequences, and this is one of them. Do you remember when we started The Mercier Press I had the same feeling? I had to do it and I did not know why. Neither do I know why today. I also recall asking you once why you loved me, and you answered: 'If I could give you the precise reasons why I love you then I would not love you at all. I would only love myself.' It is always the same. Human language is unable to explain the great mysteries of the soul. Of course I have not told everything in this book; indeed, as you know, I have left out the saddest and most painful chapters, for these things concern only ourselves, and cannot be shared with others. One day we will come face to face again, and that will be for me the day of reckoning, the final moment of truth.

Last year, 1971, was the worst year of my life. It began with your death, and the consequences which followed were far-reaching. The stupid traumatic state which I was in had all kinds of effects, social, personal, economic. I did not really mean, nor was I responsible for, nine-tenths of what I said or did, and my mind was like a jack-in-the-box, jumping and changing with every mood. That is

why I can never repay the debt I owe to people like April, Quentin, Leonore, Loretto, Dorothy and John O'Connor, Nora and Joe Barry, and above all, Maire O'Donnell. They listened with kindness and understanding to my stupid talk and silly plans, without ever once reproaching me. They knew that within a year I would find an even keel; and of course they were right, even though one part of me is lost for ever.

It was during the Christmas holidays of 1971 that I began to really balance up. I spent them with the family, and your sister Eily, at the Falls Hotel, Ennistymon, where you and I spent so many Christmasses in the past. Every stone, every path, every tree spoke to me of you. I walked along our favourite walks; I visited your old friends, your school companions, your godmother, and the school where you taught. On Christmas Day I drove the long journey to Dualla, to be with you for a few moments, to put a bunch of holly on your grave. But a calmness had descended over me and I was able to think at last. I knew I had to face life and go back into it fully; but what was also important, I had to try and undo some of the damage I caused, and the mistakes I made, during my traumatic period. I went to see people, I apologised, I explained. How kind and sympathetic they all were; some forgave me with tears in their eyes; others said: 'Welcome back, Sean, we knew you would return'. And so, back I came to life, with most of my rigging in pieces, but still afloat.

In a few months, or a few years, or a few decades, when, I do not know (but you do!), I will die too. I am no longer afraid of death. When I look at the faces of some of the living, indulgent, pained pinched and selfish, I know that to be dead cannot be as lonely as to be alive. They will lay me out in a coffin, a rosary entwined through my waxen fingers, my face pallid in the ghostly starkness of death. Friends and relatives will file past one by one, and perhaps among them there will be one discerning soul, who knew and loved me well, and who will pause and think: 'When she died, he died too. He thought he didn't, but he did. He tried hard to come back, he succeeded a little but his spirit was broken. That is why he ended his life a great might-have-been, a great failure.'

Perhaps that judgement will be correct. But who really knows? By then it will not matter anyway. I have learned from you that the only thing that really matters in life is love. All other emotions die with the body. Love lives on through all eternity. It cannot be destroyed. Side by side with you, I will be buried in Dualla. The grave will be filled in and the crowd will go for a drink in the local pubs. They will forget my faults, and they will only remember the wild and foolish pranks of my youth, when I was 'a laughing school-boy, without grief or care, riding the springy branches of an elm'. They will go home and we will both rest together, forgotten by all except our children and some few who loved us; and in a hundred years' time nobody will have ever heard of us. For this is the law of life, your universal law, to be born, to live, to suffer, to die, to be forgotten. The great storms of destiny that have swept across our lives will end, and all will be calm at last. The epitaph which I put over your grave will now serve us both:

God will wipe away all tears from their eyes;
There will be no more death and no more mourning or sadness,
The world of the past has gone.

*

Many months have passed since that day in Dualla. My plan has been partly successful; but the failures are nearly as many as the successes. For every yard I take forward, I seem to take thirty inches back, but the important thing is that I seem to be gaining a very tiny bit all the time. I foolishly thought that once I had made up my mind on what to do, everything would be simple and easy, but I was soon rudely awakened by the fact that to pass into the world of goodness, as Mary did, is a hard and painful task, especially to one who had only the broken fragments of his own worthless life to support him. It is like trying to roll a massive rock up the side of a mountain. The summit seems so far away and is mostly clouded in mist, and sometimes the ground gives way beneath me and fills me with an acute sense of despondency and even despair. There are times when I think I have found what I want and everything is clear and happy and wonderful, but then a few days later it vanishes and everything is thrown into confusion again. It seems as if my old world is dead, and the new one is refusing to be born, and I am hanging somewhere between the two. But there is no going back now. This time I cannot, and will not, fail her.

It was easier to integrate myself into my work at *The Mercier Press* than I thought it would be, for in moments of despair, I only had to remember that she founded it with me and it was closest to her heart. This set me on the right road again, and I am as deeply involved in the firm as I was when we first started it.

The discipline of writing this book was also a great help. To complete it, I had to pay a high price, in time, in patience, in concentration, and indeed sometimes in tears. I tried to follow Sidney's maxim: 'Look in thy heart and write', and I learned that one of the secrets of writing is to contemplate things until they speak themselves, and then to express them simply. Here I learned, too, that Truth serves only its slaves.

My personal life was the hardest to fit in to my plan; I found it very difficult to get used to being alone. When I went to the theatre, when I went for a walk or a drive, my continued impulse was to ring up a friend and ask him or her along. I had to resist this or else I would end up using my friends as crutches, and it was essential for me, above all, to walk without aid, to walk alone. In some of my worst moments I saw clearly that if I had died, her suffering would be terrible. In being alive I had spared her all this, and now my pain was a small price to pay. Being alone helped me to find solitude, which is one of the most glorious experiences in this world; but while solitude can be good, isolation can be bad. I went out more than ever among people, but I had now made a significant change. I no longer cultivated the company of the sophisticated, elegant people of the cities, with their futile, empty chatter. I found in the simple people, the farmers, the fishermen, the carpenters, the charwomen, the tinkers, the tailors, a rare beauty of character, a hatred of meanness and treachery, and an inherent honesty and sincerity, that I had missed since I was a child. They were the salt of the earth and I went amongst them at every opportunity.

But the pain, the sorrow, the aloneness is always there; but it is a pain of inspiration, an ecstasy of birth. Often and again I remember Nietzche's famous words: 'He who has a *why* to live can bear with almost any *how*.' It never ceases and the struggle will go on and on. It will get easier, no doubt, but I do not think it will ever end. Day by day I try to face life anew, but there is always to-morrow . . .

> *To-morrow, and to-morrow, and to-morrow,*
> *Creeps in this petty pace from day to day,*
> *To the last syllable of recorded time,*
> *And all our yesterdays have lighted fools*
> *The way to dusty death.*

To-morrow, when I finish at the office, I will walk all the way home. I will be tempted to make a detour to some favourite spot of ours, but I will resist, for I cannot live in the past or bend under the burden of memories. On the way, I will pass the second flat we had, the one where we lived when Kathleen, our first child, was born, and I will pause, and look up at the windows, and recall the days of our youth, and realise that to-day another family are starting their lives there, with hope and courage, as we did so many years before. I will remember the old saying that life attracts us with a thousand expectations, and fulfils hardly one of them. Farther on I will pass the clinic and I will see the faces of the sick, as they go in and come out, with the light of hope in their eyes and the shadow of death over their bodies, and I will remember my hope and her courage in the days that are gone. At home the house will be empty. From the back I will hear the dogs barking to attract attention; but Hoppy is dead and the others have not the same call on my affection. A photograph, a whiff of perfume, a bunch of the snowdrops she planted, will remind me of how she always waited with a smile to welcome me home no matter what the hour. I will go to the book-case and take down my favourite book of poems, *Poems to Mary*. It was written by Jonathan Hanaghan, in the weeks after the death of his wife. I will draw a chair up to the fire, and slowly I will begin to read aloud a poem which expresses everything boiling over in my bewildered, restless soul:

My ways are lone
for I am strange to many men:
my dreams are not their dreams,
and so adrift I seem
that many dread the words I speak.
I utter occult thought
that only days unborn can trace.
So when I tell my tale
they strain it through the prism of a mind
that names it blasphemy.
And thus am I to many

as a sign of dark unuttered things:
a portend of a doom they dread shall come.
And so the good deny me fellowship;
the clever, slaves to wit,
make of my earnest words a jibe.
But you my own Beloved,
gifted with a noble heart and cultured mind;
gentle and gracious, rich in tenderness;
critical and true, unknown to flattery;
did aid me from the day we pledged our love;
I never can declare your worth to me;
You counselled me to hold to my minds light
when scholared men betrayed their minds to sneer;
you bade me love them yet fulfil my trust,
to falter never yet to harden not,
and as the weight of loneliness o'ercame
you armoured me with all your woman-might
beyond your woman-strength upholding me.
Yet loyal to your love
you ceaselessly revealed to me
my falseness and my pride,
that veiled in senseless mist my primal light.
And then, Beloved,
all, all too tired with your heavy task,
you fell asleep and left me
and 'tis Night.